WILLIE GIBBS

The Hole

Book One

GPC
GIBBS PUBLISHING
CONGLOMERATE

I dedicate this book to Kinta "Big Kenny" Gibbs and to all the other friends and families out there who have lost loved ones to The Hole. And may we continue to fight for those which remain in The Hole.

"To Unlock the Mind's Unlimited Potential, One Must First Learn to Accept the Key to Creativity."

-Dameon Gibbs-

Foreword

The Hole is a powerful and thought-provoking work of literature that immediately captures the reader's attention, vividly portraying the challenges inner-city youth face in their struggle to escape its grip. It brings a new and refreshing take on the genre of urban writing, as it perfectly blends autobiography with compelling storytelling. **The Hole** neither hides nor attempts to dress up the notion of drug violence as it might be shown on the silver screen. Due to the author's detailed description of his lifestyle, readers must be aware of the maturity level needed to endure such a graphic novel; but, do not allow his candid approach to deter you from storytelling at its best.

The Hole will open your eyes to a lifestyle many believe they thought they knew. **The Hole** describes a life which is harsh and brutal, while simultaneously delivering stories of love, hope, and determination to those who are in need of encouragement.

Reading this young man's journey through life, readers will come to understand the true meaning of hate, love, pain, joy, captivity, freedom, struggle and determination. May your journey into the shadows of **The Hole** be as thrilling one. May a stray ray of light from these pages open your eyes to a world constantly hidden from view. So, prepare yourself for a roller coaster ride as you enter into **The Hole**.

Dameon Gibbs
    -Author and Historian-

Preface

This book contains events which happened in my life and thus is not a fictitious work. The people and locations may have been altered to protect the privacy of those who wish not to be named. However, the events which take place are as real as they come, and for this reason, I refuse to tell them as if they were some happily ever after fairytale. Simply sitting down to write what this book contains took a kind of energy I never knew I had. Creating it has transformed my life, and I hope it offers you a new perspective as you sit and read. I will do my best to keep it simple by narrating and describing to you my life as if you were sitting before me when I was living it. No filler, no filter, and no pretend love drama like modern writers are doing. My goal is to provide the truth and reality of life on the streets through my eye as I lived it in **The Hole**.

Acknowledgments

I wish to acknowledge my son Will Gibbs for being my inspiration to be a better man and ultimately to be a better father.

I would also like to give special thanks to JB for dedicating hours with helping us bring this series into reality.

Special thanks to all my family and friends who kept hope in me and helped me to see through all the rough years I have been through.

Thanks to all those who helped jog my memory on various events, if it were not for you this work could not have been possible.

Last but far from being least, I thank God for His love and guidance, and for believing in me when I did not see a way out **The Hole**.

BOOK I: THE LIFE, THE STRUGGLE & THE TRUTH

CHAPTER ONE: THE QUESTION

I never intended on ever writing a book, especially the one you are taking the time to read now. However, this changed in the year 2012 when I was in what some might call a financial rut, with no job, with no money, with no occupation and simply down on my luck because no employer would hire me due to my legal background. It was a place I came to call **The Hole**.

One day on a cold winter evening when I was spending time with my fifteen-year-old son, he asked me one simple question. And though it was a simple question, it was an important question. It was a simple question for which I did not have a simple answer to give. So, to answer his question I came up with what you are about to begin, starting with Book One in a series of five books. A series which would answer his question in its entirety in BOOK FIVE. He might not understand everything I describe at his current age, but I pray as he matures, the full meaning of the series will be revealed to him.

Also, by the end of reading the series, I hope you ask yourself, would your answer be any different than the answer I gave my son?

However, before I start my story about life in **The Hole,** I want to say first God comes for all of us, promising nothing more in life except one day you will die. There is no promise for success, no promise of wealth, no promise for happiness, love or health. The only thing for certain in life is death. It is what you do between life and death which determines where you will spend eternity. A man's character brings him certain consequences, as well as certain rewards. Now unless a man regret being a man, he should accept his consequences like a man, as he gracefully accepts his rewards.

CHAPTER TWO: THE HERITAGE

Here is a little story I must tell you about me, a story I know all too well. Thus, making it the best means of answering your question son. It started way back in history with my two great and unforgettable parents and your grandparents, Levi and Kayden Carter.

My parents met in the early 1970's. They knew the same folks but did not know each other until a mutual friend by the name of Yancy Davis introduced them. They hit it off pretty well right at the beginning. My Mom Kayden Hill (her maiden name at the time), was fifteen years old and my Pop Levi Carter was only eighteen years old. Yancy was dating my Aunt Skylar Carter, and this is how he was introduced to the Carter family. As a friend to both the Carters and Hills, I believe fate brought the two families together—forever changing their lives.

Back in the 70's all of the kids in the neighborhood got along pretty well—not like you kids today who do not get along because the other one might be wearing different colored shoes. There was no foolishness like that.

Anyway, my mom and pop started hanging out more frequently—and when I say frequently, I mean nearly every day and night. Eventually, they came to a point in their relationship where they laid down to enjoy each other, and to-do-the-do. My pops, or should I say, my father, wanted a nut, and that's exactly what he got, a *nut*.... I was made! Now myself, I think this is kind of awesome! But some may later see it as a curse.

With perfect timing or of an unbelievable consequence, my mother Kayden Hill went into labor on my father's birthday of October 3rd. As he was born October 3, 1957, and I was born October 3, 1975. In case you did not see it, if you turn the last two digits around on the year, everything would be the same. We were nearly numerical twins. But this is not the end to this crazy number game my father and I share.

Now my father's name is Levi Carter 3rd and me; I am Levi Carter III. Notice the difference with the suffix on both names, Crazy Right!? My father and I shared the same birthday, with matching suffixes spoken differently. However, this still isn't the end of it.

We also shared the same Social Security Number. And this alone always had me thinking, WOW! How often does this sort of thing happen in the world? The Government must have run out of all numbers on this one day or something because this is one of the most ridiculous numbers games I have ever come across to date. All the numbers in our Social Security Numbers are the same, except for the last digit, for his ended with 4 and mine ended with 5. And when I first learned of this, it was cool; it was something I shared with everyone. I did not realize the importance of it or how it would change my life, but I would not come to learn of this until I was older, and I will go into detail of this when the time presents itself later.

So here we have the same birthday's, he was Levi Carter 3rd, and I was Levi Carter III. Truthfully, I do not understand how the doctors did not catch this. And to top it off, we both have the same Social Security Number, except for the last digit. *Craziness.*

After my birth into this world of ours, my parents go on to have three more sons over the next six years or so. Their names from oldest to youngest are Anthony, Quinton, and Dominic. It was no longer all about me anymore; my reign had ended, as my brother Anthony, or Tucker as we called him, wanted to share in my spoiling with his birth in 1976. *Hahaha.* Three years after his birth, he picked up the nickname Tucker. Why, I never figured out—but it was there, and it stuck with him his entire life.

In 1979 Quinton was added to the mix, he eventually picked up the name Quick. Quick had something to do with him being fast as a child, and like Tucker, his nickname simply stuck with him to this day.

Three years later in 1982 the youngest boy was born, Dominic Carter. It was something my parents liked about the number three because they were all three years apart. Yeah, I know, my parents and their crazy number play right? My mother had four boys and no girls.

Let me pump my brakes here for a minute. I should have informed you of this at the beginning, my mother had one sister by the name of Evelyn Davis. And my Aunt Evelyn is an awesome person, but she uses to mess with this crazy nigga name Blake McCall. Blake uses to run and hang with my father and his siblings back in the day. As for my father he had four sisters: Valencia-Burton, Skylar Carter, Regina 'Crazy Ass' Carter, and Faith Roberts.

Ok, are you still with me? I know I threw a lot of names at you, but it's all necessary to answer his question. Ok, so let's move along. Like I said, my Aunt Evelyn and Blake kicked it and had a son name Raw, but they named him after Blake. Blake already had a son name Blake McCall Jr., so Raw became Blake McCall 3rd. There goes the number 3 again, *Hahaha*. Raw was born February 3, 1975. We called Blake McCall 3rd, Lil Raw! He got the name because they say his little ass was always trying to lick or eat raw food. I'm telling you, something was seriously wrong with the little boy. But anyway!

Now on my father's side, like I said, my father had four sisters and one funny ass brother, Melvin Burton. But we later called him "The Hideous Unk," because he is one scary ass nigga.

Valencia had three kids from oldest to youngest: Stan, Candy, and Lisa, who I came to call Lee-Lee.

Melvin had four kids, three girls and one boy. Their names are Dana, Mitchell, Christian Burton and Melvin Burton Jr.

My Aunt Skylar had two kids, one son and one daughter by my father's homeboy Yancy, but she already had one daughter name, Hailey Blackwell. The kids she had by Yancy were Yancy Davis jr. but we called his ass Murphy and his sister Orenda Davis.

My Aunt Regina had no kids but adopted everyone else and helped out whenever and however she could.

That got damn Aunt of mine named Faith had five damn kids, one girl, and four boys. Starting with the one girl there was Vanessa than Faith's four boys: Bruce, Ralph, Bobby and Joseph.

Now before all the bad things started and before crack took over our streets in the 80's, my family was TIGHT! Nothing could separate us, which is something many families are missing nowadays. Anyway, let me now fast-forward this a little to the 80's.

CHAPTER THREE: THE BEGINNINGS

Baltimore, Maryland, back in the early 80's was wild. In most, or should I say on all of the urban neighborhoods, there was dope and crack being dealt on every street corner. On top of everything, there were the neighborhood gangs. B-more, as we and others like to call it, 'Murda-land'! I don't know how we ran the streets of B-more and went to school every day without missing a day. This was a miracle by itself.

Everybody had their grind and day to day activities. My parents went to work Monday through Friday, doing the nine to five thing and had the weekends to party, party, party. And when I say party, I mean they had music bumping, liquor, beer pouring, reefers going up in smoke, and cocaine to polish it off. This was happening all over the house while we, the kids were supposed to be in our bedrooms, away from the adults.

Haha, I laughed at the thought of staying in my room, for simply telling me to stay there was not enough to make me do it. I was a nosey little sucker! I used to sneak out my room every chance I got to see how my parents partied. I remember sneaking out of the room for the first time and finding them sniffing some white powder off a mirror using a little straw. And to accompany this white power they passed around reefer and alcohol, all while dancing to Kurtis Blow's: *If I Ruled the World*.

It was wild. It was like something you would see in a movie. All I knew was I wanted to get older so I could do the same thing. Why would I want anything else? They were having a good time dancing, laughing and living life to the fullest. Seeing those parties transpire became a dream of mine, I wanted to experience it, watching them, the seeds of drugs and partying had been planted.

Although my parents were into the drugs and partying, they continued to do their duties of being parents as best they thought fit. Meaning they stayed together as a couple the entire time, as my brothers and I grew up.

Now Saturday was our day, like most kids, every Saturday morning we watched cartoons, and had breakfast which consisted either of grits, bacon, scrapple, pancakes, cereal, oatmeal or a good old syrup sandwich. Yeah, syrup sandwiches were a staple in our household. And the best syrup sandwiches were made from King's syrup. King Syrup was thick as peanut butter and stuck to ribs like glue. You may laugh at what we had, but it got us through the day.

Unlike you kids nowadays, after eating we went outside and played, there were no video games or at least ones we could afford. So we had to make our own fun happen. After breakfast on Saturdays, a group of friends of mine from around the neighborhood would meet up at various locations where we had placed dirty ass mattresses.

We did not care how dirty these mattresses were; we were kids. And from sun up to sundown, we would flip and play all sorts of games on them. One hour it may be seeing how high we could jump, trying to touch the sky. The next it would be how many summersaults we could do in the air before landing back on the mattress. My brothers' favorite game to play was when we lined nine of the mattresses in a row, one end in front the other. And running as fast we could bounce on the first mattress, we saw how far we would sail down the line of mattresses before landing.

We all learned how to do a backward summersault twist on those mattresses. Those were the good old days. Eventually, there came a time when we no longer needed the mattresses because we had learned how to flip on concrete. This was usually done in the middle of the street when cars were not coming. We chose to flip in the streets because they tended to be a little cleaner than other areas. I can only smile at how my brothers, and I grew up so close. Matter of fact, the whole family was close knit. I can sit here and remember the days sitting at my father and mother's side, *Ahh we were all so close.*

There were other times when my cousin Raw and I would play in the old houses on Parrish Street. Parrish Street was a little street behind both my grandmothers' houses. My mother's mother, Laura, lived on Winchester Street and my father's mother, Inas, lived around the corner on Stricker Street. During those days, I was a little firebug who loved setting things on fire.

One day I did the same thing I normally do which was set something on fire and watch it burn. However, on this particular day, the fire did not do what I wanted it to. This time, I decided to set fire to some old cords in the walls, but the wall was right by the stove's gas line. When I finally got the fire going as I wanted, I nearly burned down the entire block of Parrish Street. Yeah, it was stupid, but you could not tell me anything. I was young and dumb. My little brothers were not with me at the time of these fires, but if they were, Oh Well!

Once the fires became larger, Raw and I would run away and more often than not, the older folks would see us. They would yell at us saying things like, "I'm going to tell your parents when I see them because Y'all know better!" Deep down inside we knew if the old folks could've gotten their hands on Raw & I, they would have beat the holy shit out of us themselves. And after they whooped our butts, they would have taken us to our parents only for them to give us another ass whooping. Back in those days, it was nothing for other adults to beat your ass without your parent's permission. It was like an unwritten consent!

It was during these years when Raw and I grew closer, forming a bond still going strong today. Man, it's amazing to think about the things we used to get into—catching grasshoppers, yellow jackets, bumblebees, spiders, praying mantises, or snakes. No matter what we were doing, we had to make sure it was all done before nightfall, which meant being back on the steps before the streetlights came on. If we did not make it back before the streetlights came on, it was an automatic *ASS WHOOPING*. As in it being a guarantee. And you did not have an ass whooping until you had a Grandma Laura ass whooping.

Raw didn't live with us, but every time we went to Grandma Laura's house, he was always there. Now Grandma Laura did not play around at all, and although she knew how to use a belt or switch like a pastor knows how to use his Bible, she was still so sweet. She would beat your ass, feed your ass, and follow it with giving your ass money to play outside because she did not want you in the house looking at her.

Evelyn, Raw's mother, stopped dating Blake, and eight years later she met a man name, Johnny Johnson. My aunt and Mr, J.J as we called him, short for his two initials, had two daughters: Kendra and Zaneta Johnson. Aunt Evelyn having a new man, and more children did not stop Raw and me from being little bad asses. Raw and I were considered to be the smarter ones out of the group. Not saying the younger ones were dumb or anything like it, but we were more focused on finding ways to have fun. Man, Raw and I were two of a kind.

I remember when Raw and I were playing in Grandma Laura's house on Winchester Street, when Raw did the dumbest thing ever, by knocking over an entire can of paint down the interior steps. The thing is, Grandma had recently installed new burgundy carpet with beige pattern streaks throughout the house.

Normally we did not play in the house, but I think we were punished for fighting each other outside the day before. I do not know what the hell made the jackass play with the paint in Grandma Laura's house anyway! Nonetheless on the steps. Raw stupid ass took off the paint lid and was looking at it curiously. He stuck his finger in it and wiped it on my arm. When I tried to stick my finger in the can of paint to get him back, he jumped up and knocked the can over.

As the paint spilled down the stairs onto Grandma's new carpet, the world appeared to have slowed down. I looked Raw straight in his eyes, for I wanted to remember my cousin as he was. Because I knew when Grandma found out this shit right here, Blake McCall 3rd was going to be FUBAR. Fucked Up Beyond All Recognition. Raw was going to die today and the sad thing is, he knew it as well.

This guy looked at me with an expression saying only one thing, *Will please help me!* This nigga was scared for dear life. Raw was my cousin so I figured I would help him clean up the paint. Now Raw was the slick trickster. He held the bag while I got up the paint, and when we finished, I was the only one who had paint all over me, and my man Raw was spotless. I mean he was clean as a whistle.

We got up the mess before grandma found out about the paint. However, it was now time for dinner, and I could not miss dinner. So I sucked it up like a man or should I say, I tried to suck it up like a man and went to dinner with paint all over me.

"Boy I know you weren't in the paint," were Grandma Laura's first words.

Man, I looked over at Raw, who was standing nearby with no paint on him. Looking at him with an innocent look on his face, the first thing I could think of was, *this little sucker*. I turned back to my grandma who was still looking at me, waiting for an answer, without saying a word I felt my knees turn to Jello.

And with a look which had to be dumb, I responded, "No I wasn't in no paint."

You would have thought I punched her in the mouth or something simply because of the way she looked at me. I turned to Raw, hoping he would vouch for me on this one since I helped him.

But remember, I said Raw was the smart one. The first thing he said was, "Yes you were."

Why are all kid's favorite words when they are trying to get themselves out of trouble? "Yes, you were."

Anyway, Grandma got up after Raw had lied on me about knocking over the paint can down her stairs. Man-o-man......my ass still hurt from the whooping she decided to deposit on me that day. And don't get me wrong, I did not have the luxury of being beaten with a belt like most kids around the neighborhood. No, no, she decided to use a freaking fishing rod to get the work done. While she was whooping my ass, all I could think about was, *where in the hell did, she get a fishing rod from? Was she planning on going fishing today?* Beats me, all I know was it came out of nowhere, and it was like having lightning on a nice shiny new leather belt because my poor cheeks were burning with each crack from her swing.

But what made matters even worse was the fact I got another beating by my mom when she came home. Yeah, in those days, if you did something wrong, you faced consequences from every member of the household until, as a group, they decided you had suffered enough. Punishment was real back in the day. The little time kids spend in their rooms nowadays is nothing compared to before, and on top of it, today many of them still get to watch television.

I could not beat Raw up like I originally wanted to for what he had done. So, I had to get on his level and fight back, for I was not going to let this one slide. Two beatings and two punishments in one day was enough to make me do about anything. I thought long and hard about how to get his butt back. I finally came up with the idea of eating all of Grandma Laura's chicken she made for dinner. And believe me, I made sure to give Raw a piece before all the chicken was gone. Man, my plan was coming together perfectly because he smashed on the chicken.

Whenever Grandma Laura got in the kitchen, it was magical. Grandma Laura could always make something delicious out of nothing. Granny grew up in the south, and she had the most beautiful hands to produce some beautiful meals. I loved to watch her make homemade bread or biscuits. She learned to cook from her mother & grandmother she told me. And her repertoire was mainly Southern.

Now on this particular day when Grandma was in her lab as she would say, she was making Southern Fried Chicken. And if you were outside, you were able to smell the fried chicken all the way down the street. It probably took Granny maybe an hour and a half to make the meal. She made dinner pretty early — it was always ready before the 5:00 pm news came on.

Grandma Laura would go upstairs into her room to watch the news. Now, for some reason, Raw thought I had forgotten the ass whooping Granny gave me because of what he did. It's been damn near three weeks since Raw knocked the can of paint down the stairs. But as they saying goes, revenge is a dish better-served cold, and today Raw would meet his fate. Every day since he set me up to take the fall for him over the spilled paint, I planned to get Raw back. That punk ass nigga was scared straight the day he knocked the paint over, but I took the charge for him.

So today would be like no other because when Grandma Laura went to her room to watch the news, I took nine pieces of chicken, and I ate 8 of them. Oh, best believe I made sure Granny didn't know, or it would be a murder at 1515 Winchester Street.

"Hey, Raw!" I carefully called out. "Do you want this last piece of chicken?" And just like I thought he said, "Yeah."

Raw ate the chicken like it was his last meal. "Well, it might have been once Grandma found out he ate all the chicken. As he sat there with chicken crumbs and grease all around his lips, I simply laughed in my head, thinking, *Aww he's gonna get it.*

My plan worked flawlessly. When Grandma Laura came downstairs after watching her TV shows, the first thing she screamed upon seeing the chicken was gone was, "Who in the hell ate all the chicken?"

I made sure I was right by her side to witness this event firsthand and to see the expression on his face was going to be priceless. I immediately answered, "Raw had some chicken a few minutes ago. I thought you gave him a few pieces, and he gave me some."

Man, when I say she beat all the living hell out of him, she beat all the living hell out of him. The little self-satisfying smirk he wore in the weeks before was all but gone. Replaced with the same look I had on my face when he had lied on me about the paint. And if he did not lie on me the first time, I would have felt sorry for him. She beat him like she was a rug cleaner, because in her mind Raw should have known better.

Now these were only a few incidents Raw, and I experienced growing up in the Sandtown neighborhood. But when it came to growing up with my brothers and living in the same house, it was a totally different and harder experience than growing up being Raw's younger cousin. Having little brothers, who acted up in the house, and me being the oldest, was like having my personal boarding pass to *Whoopington Town*. And each new day seemed to bring a host of new whoopings and punishments.

We did not go over Grandma Laura's house this one week. We were punished this particular weekend, and thinking about it, we were some bad ass children being raised at our address on 1613 W. Mulberry Street in a three-floor house.

In one scenario my two brothers Tucker and Quick got into a fight. They could be no older than seven and eight years old. They always fought, as brothers tend to do. I am not exactly sure what they were fighting over because

I was not there, all I know is Tucker got a beating behind something Quick did. Quick was next to the youngest. Anyway, when Tucker got an ass whooping from Pops before they were both sent to their room. When Tucker went to sleep that night, Quick dumped gasoline all over the side of the bed Tucker was sleeping on. He lit it on fire, trying to scare, hurt, or maybe even kill Tucker — or at least, that's what I've always believed. Terrible! Hell yeah, we were some bad ass kids.

Our Father beat Quick with a boat paddle after they got the fire under control. Yes, I said a mutha fucking boat paddle! I wanted to call the police on my father sometimes for his abuse towards us, but I was afraid they would let his ass out on bail or something.

My mother Kayden did not say anything when Levi beat us. She thought we deserved everything that came our way. It didn't help us any knowing our parents were addicted to cocaine. Following the episode, Tucker and Quick stopped speaking to each other for maybe a day. The next day we were up looking for something else to break or disrupt. No matter how bad Levi would whip us, we would still find the energy to fuck up some more shit in the house or outside. We were some bad ass kids, and nobody wanted us to stay over their house.

Now when it came down to the youngest, Dominic, the only thing my Pop had to do was pull his belt off and ask Dominic, who we nicknamed Nick, "Who did what?" Basically, asking Nick to snitch, if Nick did not snitch, he would slap Nick to get him to tell, that is once Nick was a little older, maybe around the age of six or eight. Funny thing now that I look back on it is that he would slap the hell out of Nick so he would tell him what had happened. And after Nick had spilled the truth, he would have to slap him again to get him to shut the hell up.

We were so bad sometimes we would get punished for the entire year, not really, but there were times we would be in the house for months because of the dumb shit we did. Some would say my Pops was hard on us, but in all truth, it helped make me who I am today.

Now, this was about my bad ass brothers and me; however, there's also the other side of the family I want to talk about, like my cousins. The time or should I say the year was 1986. The hip-hop groups were LL Cool J, Run DMC, EPMD, KRS1, Salt & Pepper, Beastie Boyz and Biz Markie to name a few.

My cousins on my father's side of the family consisted mainly of girls except for Stan, who was the oldest of us all, and my cousin Murphy. Murphy was younger than me but still old enough for me to chill with. Now Stan did not have a whole lot of rap for me. I contribute this to him being in a league of his own. And when I say a league, I mean hustling — a league I wasn't part of. And to tell the truth, in my mind, I always wanted to be like my Big Cousin Stan. He had all the hottest women, the coolest clothes, and the waves that spin. You know the kind of hair that makes you feel motion sickness if you stare too long. And man, do women love a man with waves.

But the one thing I could not stand about Stan was the fact he did not speak to me, nor to my brothers. He used to walk right by us with his gold chains around his neck; this is family I am talking about. If you only knew how it felt for this to happen, having your so-called icon pass by you without saying a word. Maybe he did not speak to us because we were not wearing the coolest things like Guess Jeans, Bill Blast Jeans, Levi Jeans, Bike's sweatpants or maybe Nike's, Puma's, or Diador's.

Now my brothers and I had on the phony shit, the shit people in school laughed at us about. The shit which got your ass whooped after school type of shit. We had on Uncle Charlie Jeans, brown corduroy or Lee's jeans. People used to call Lee's "Shouts!" and there was a little jingle about Shouts that people sang, like the song, "Shout Shout by Tears for Fear" when they start dissing you. 1 Anyway I do not have much of a singing voice but here goes the song, *"Shout......Shout your Lee's are played out, these are the pants I can do without....so Shout on, I'm talking to you. Shout On!"* "Man, I couldn't stand the song, as you can see how it stuck with me all these years.

But to keep matters moving, none of our shirts were name brand. Stan had on Polo shirts. We had on what I call, *don't know's*. But we matched, and if somebody said something about our outfits, they got punched in the face.

While our parents struggled to keep clothes on our backs, Stan stayed fly. But I believe it was the drugs which kept my parents from buying us things. All their money was going straight to the drug man. There were several moments

I remember when we had to move out of a house because my father owed the drug man the equivalent of several months of rent. And when the drug man came to collect his funds, my father only had one option, TO PAY HIM! When you owe the drug man, you better pay up or suffer the consequences. If not, the dope man would send in his enforcer to beat you like you were a rag doll. Pistol whipping was often an effective means of getting a point across. I once saw a lady get pistol whipped, and it was not a pretty sight.

Now when I turned ten or eleven, I started to learn the streets were a nightmare. By this time, we were always moving from house to house, and I didn't know why. It wasn't until I was a little older when I learned the truth. We were not moving; we were getting evicted because the rent money was going up my parents' noses from the cocaine usage.

With no other place to live, we were all forced to move in with my father's mother Inas Carter, or Grandma Inas as my brothers and me came to call her. We lived in her basement at 1160 North Stricker Street in a three-story house.

We now lived in the slums of Baltimore, judging by the look of the neighborhood. "R.I.P." signs in front of names and gang graffiti covered the area. All six of us—Levi, Kayden, Tucker, Quick, Nick, and me—stayed in a rat-infested basement. When we came around my father's side of the family, they treated us wrong. They treated us like we were lower than them; looking down on us like we were dirty and funky. To them, we might have been worse than the homeless. Like anyone else, I hate the way they treated us, but one day I knew it had to change.

The funny thing about this situation was when our father was around them, they did not treat us the same way. Fake Mutha Fuckers! Everything was supposedly all chocolate and cupcakes. I believe we were treated badly because we were not fly like the other grandkids. However, they were smart enough to not treat us shady around Levi because they understood he had a horrible temper. And would have most likely beat someone down for teasing his kids. Levi, I know for sure, would have gone off on somebody or hurt someone if they tried him, as he was more often than not, high.

However, my mother noticed this change and how my father's side was treating us differently from their kids. I can remember one incident where my Aunt Faith beat the shit out of my brother Tucker when he was about ten, before she told him to get his dirty ass out the house.

Tucker was the type even at a young age who did not take crap from anyone, especially if he felt they were doing him wrong. Standing his ground, Tucker locked eyes with her and said, "I'm not dirty like you!"

You might not understand this, but in those days talking back to an adult was taboo, it's something you simply did not do. It was almost a law if you talked back or disrespected an adult, the adult had a right to discipline you. But on this day, Tucker did not care about this unwritten law and felt he had to stand up for himself.

In that moment Faith beat the FUCK out of my brother. She slapped him first; then punched him square in the jaw before . she grabbed Tucker by his collar, only to throw him out in the backyard. Not finish with him, she went and beat on Tucker some more in the yard, not to mention stomping on his smaller body.

After the beating, he received from my aunt, Tucker had no choice but to tell my mother. And before my mother had the opportunity to go back upside Faith's head, my father intervened. Telling my mother to take us and go live with Grandma Laura around the corner on Winchester Street.

My Mom did not like the idea of us moving with Grandma Laura for three reasons: 1.) Faith was going to get away with beating her child, not simply disciplining him for doing something wrong, but beating him like he was an adult. 2.) The family was being split up for the first time, as my father was very involved in our childhood. 3.) She did not get the chance to lay an ass whooping on Faith for beating her child.

We being kids did not mind the move, we were often seen as the trouble kids of the family by many of my father's relatives. And we figured life would be much different living with Grandma Laura. But do not get me wrong, Grandma Laura offered a new series of whooping, as I explained previously with the spilled paint.

Although my father handled his responsibilities as a father, things instantly begin to change once we moved out of my Grandma Inas' basement. Levi soon fell deeper into drugs. Sniffing coke as if there were a shortage of it. Was this a reaction to him attempting to deal with the family crisis, being stuck in the middle? His children's mother and children on one side, and his mother, brother and sisters on the other? How do you choose in a situation like that? Or did his drug use increase because he no longer had kids around to look out for? And freedom was all his to grasp!

Whatever the case may be, my father became a heavy cokehead, and to top it off, he started selling to stay ahead of his coke habit. And ahead he got, as money started flowing into his hand. I remember times when he would send me to the store to get two packs of sunflower seeds with a hundred-dollar bill, which happened to be one of his favor snacks. Now ask yourself, what adult would send a thirteen-year-old to a store with a hundred-dollar bill to buy two packs of sunflower seeds which cost less than a dollar a piece? Someone Fucking High with lots of money! He would be so coked up common sense simply did not matter. But with all the hundreds of dollars he had, we never received the sort of things our cousins did. I never figured out why he did not buy us name brand things. I guess it's the same today as it used to be. All drug dealers damn near stingy as hell. But despite his highness, those days were some of the bests, because he never asked for change his change back.

My mom was a user of the white powder too but was not as deep into it as he was. You may sit back and judge my parents for their so-called lack of parenting, yet if you look at it from a past perspective, it was a part of the neighborhood culture back. For some odd reason, it appears to me the behavior was more accepted in the past compared to today. Whether this is the case or not, I am not sure. I am simply giving you my perspective; with this, knowing I am not condoning anyone's actions.

Anyway, once the situation went down with my Aunt Faith fucking Tucker up, my mother came to a drastic and sudden turning point in her life. When we moved with my Grandma Laura at her three bedrooms, two story house on Winchester Street, my brothers and I had to sleep in the same bed. I do not know what prompted my mother, maybe it was a guilty lifestyle, but it was during this time she began informing Grandma Laura of everything unfolding around Grandma Inas' house. Telling her about all the alcohol, drugs, and the money.

I do not know if I ever mentioned the fact my Grandma Inas and Grandma Laura were like sisters at one point. I am not sure if they ever exchanged words on the matter, but whatever the case was, their relationship continued, nonetheless.

Now Grandma Laura used to live by a small little church on Winchester Street called *Temple of Christ Baptist Church*. The Reverend's wife, Mother Sue used to come to my grandma's house often to check on her. One day, Grandma Laura introduced Mother Sue to my mother. I am not sure how Mother Sue went so long without knowing my mother in the first place being Mother Sue talked to Grandma Laura all the time. But this particular day was different as Mother Sue happened to notice in my mother, something my mother probably did not see in herself. On this day, she invited my mother to one of their upcoming services. And as we like to say, Mother Sue laid them 'Godly Hands' on Mom for prayer, after which, it was all she wrote. From that moment on, my mother immediately left all the drugs behind her.

Now it's the spring of 1988, and my mother Kayden has been drug-free for two years and is now an active member of *Temple of Christ Baptist Church*. Being she was practicing the whole idea of forgiveness; she started allowing my brothers and me to visit Grandma Inas' house again. It was from this moment when things start to get a little interesting: My father is still getting high, yet my mom, my brothers, and I still love him.

The family being split up a few years and our father not being around as much began to take its toll on the family. Over time, the fights between Tucker and Quick increased, becoming more frequent, and were not isolated to our home.

One time while they were in school, and during the middle of the school day, Tucker left his classroom while the teacher was in the middle of her lesson. He went to Quick's class, walked in and popped the living shit out of him in front his peers. And although Quick was the younger brother, he was no softy, but overall, he was still no match for Tucker's size. The two of them got to rumbling in the classroom like they were worst enemies, knocking tables and chairs all around the room while their peers watched.

Tucker laid a beat down on Quick that day, and when they came home from school after being suspended, my mom laid the beat down on both them and top it off with them being grounded. With me being the oldest, I did not appreciate how it all went down when I heard what Tucker did to Quick. The fight was all over Quick joking how Tucker was becoming a sloppy fat boy. Quick had all Tucker's friends laughing at him.

I went to Tucker and said, "I bet you won't do me like that."

And before he could even respond or prepare himself, I punched him in the face, knocking him to the ground. When Tucker tried to get back up to fight me back, Quick started stomping Tucker. Now it was like an all-out street brawl as Quick, and I jump Tucker. Eventually, all the stomping became loud enough for my mother to hear, she came running into the bedroom. Bursting the door open, she found Quick and me dealing with our brother as though he had broken into our house. Seeing mom, we stopped and allowed Tucker to get up off the floor.

My Mom did not waste any time to lay down another round of spankings on us all. Tucker was as hardheaded as he could be and was not trying to go down like Quick and I did. But he did what we called getting 'swole up,' or sticking out his chest so to speak to Mom. She noticed he was attempting to stand up to her, and she was not going to have it. Man, when I say she 'wild out' on him, I mean she 'wild out' on him. This day was simply not going Tucker's way. He had been fighting all day, first with Quick in school, came home to be beaten by Mom, jumped by Quick and me, and now he was getting the breaks beat off his ass yet again. On this day, I wished my brother wasn't so hardheaded; this whooping was nearly worse than the one Faith gave him. Mom must have forgotten he was her child.

After the ass whooping of all ass whoopings, she sent Tucker back around Grandma Inas' house to live with our father. Good thing for Tucker, my father was out of town on another one of his drug runs—if it can be considered a good thing. Either way, Tucker's beating stopped on that day. So, while my father was out of town, Tucker was forced to stay around the corner at Grandma Inas' house until he returned.

Now Grandma Inas' house was much larger than Grandma Laura's house, but it was no luxury mansion either. It was a three-story brick row home, which was typical for the Baltimore Sandtown area in the 1980's. On the third floor lived my Aunt Faith in the front room and Aunt Regina had the back room. On the second floor was Grandma Inas in the front room, Uncle Melvin stayed in the back room, and the bathroom separated the two of them.

The first floor, from front to back, included the living room, dining room, a half bathroom in the middle, and the kitchen at the end. My father had no choice but to live in his mother's basement after we were evicted from our last house at *1613 w. Mulberry Street.* He had no choice but to sleep in the basement because there was no way Grandma Laura was going to allow him stay around there with us on Winchester Street.

So, owing to his drug habit and not paying rent on Mulberry Street, Levi had to sleep in the basement. I do not know how he tolerated living in the basement; it was cold and damp. However, the worst thing was in the fact it was rat infested. I mean big, big rats. City rats, the healthy ones the size of cats.

Talking about the rats, I remember there was a time when Levi would get so damn high and while sitting in the basement, he would start shooting at the damn rats with his .357 as they scurried about. Honestly, to this day I do not understand why nobody ever called the police on him because got damn, he shot a damn gun in the house. He was a crazy man.

But back to the story, my brother Tucker made it so hard on himself he had to sleep in the basement by himself. I guess not really by himself; he did have my father's rat friend, Ben, running around. For the first few days, I did not go around Grandma Inas' house to see him, but my little brother Nick did. Nick would check on Tucker and come back and tell us Tucker was doing OK. And truth be told I was glad to hear he was because I knew he did not want to be around there with rats.

After several days had passed, Nick came running from around the corner, after being at Grandma Inas' house and told us our cousins and aunts were around there. Now this was my chance to become cool with Tucker after Quick, and I jumped him. Man, when we turned the corner, it was like a block party was going on. And unlike boring Winchester Street, people were sitting on their front steps laughing, talking, with music bumping from nearly every house. The first thing I did after turning the corner was locate Tucker and make up with him. Good thing it was not a hard thing to do, I found him playing with a group of kids from the neighborhood.

When I approached him, he acted like nothing ever happened. He simply asked if I wanted to play with them, and of course I did not hesitate to say, "Yeah." I think I would go crazy if something tragic ever happened to my brother.

I remember the day like it was yesterday; it was one of my best childhood days. First thing first, I made up with Tucker, who I did not talk to in days, let alone see. And second, my brothers and I were back together having fun as brothers should do. When I tell you the day was so fun, boy oh boy, it really was. It was a perfect spring day, warm and bright. And we kids took total advantage of it as we played in the fire hydrant and ran up and down the streets playing Catch One-Catch All and Hide and Seek. Although I enjoyed playing Catch One-Catch All, Hide and Seek was still my favorite game to play.

Of course, the grownups did their own thing, running in and out of the house doing what grownups did. I do not know how I was able to notice as I played with my friends, but somehow, I watched as my father's car pulled up. Levi drove a four door, brown 1985 Ford Thunderbird. I can clearly picture this, as I remember the world seemingly slowing down. At first, I thought something had happened to my father because I only saw his friend Dennis driving. After Dennis parked the car, my father opens the passenger door and ran into the house.

At the time it was strange, and I did not give it too much thought. However, as I got older, I learned why Levi was hiding in the car before running into the house. It was because he had 5 bricks of cocaine on him. It was all about getting in the house without being caught. And good thing he did not get caught, because if he did, I probably would have never seen him again. This all makes me wonder, what my already screwed up family would have done, even more, how things would have turned out without him?

Nevertheless, our cousin Candy was over from Irvington Avenue for the block party. Irvington Avenue no means better than the neighborhood I was living in. Her neighborhood had the same drug dealers, drug addicts, and gangs. The only difference might have been they were a little cleaner.

The one other thing which sticks with me from that day, besides making up with Tucker and my father returning, was this moment when Candy came over, bringing her pretty ass friend, Felesha. Felesha was what every nigga, drug dealer, or glue head in the neighborhood wanted or at least hoped to get. Felesha was a tight fit, fair-skinned, with long hair dark as coal, and the most beautiful hazel eyes. She wore a tight fit yellow Nike T-shirt with Mickey & Minnie Mouse printed on the front wearing gold chains. The Jordache jeans she had on complimented her curves. Got damn Flesha was awesome! How did this girl's parents let their thirteen-year-old daughter out the house with the way she dressed? She had on Nike Air Max, which ran about $95, this alone made me wonder if I was enough for her.

Her very presence demanded attention on a whole new level. However, there was one problem, she was used to being around them dudes around her way with money, money I did not have. No money meant she was by no means checking me out. But because I did not have the money or was not fresh, did not mean I could not try to get her attention. I tried to be like my big cousin Stan, who kept his hair cut and brushed at all times like it was someone's summer lawn, and having a fresh cut meant I needed more money.

Everyone was having so much fun Felesha stayed the entire day with us, a day I intended to use to my advantage of getting to know her. And if I knew one thing about girls, it was if you wanted them, you had to make them smile and smiling did I keep her the entire day.

I had to make an ass of myself, but it worked. And by ass, I mean literally taking off all my clothes and putting on a trench coat to come outside naked. From time to time throughout the day, I would open my coat unexpectedly and flash Felesha, doing a little up and down jiggle, ensuring she saw all the goodies. Although I was young, I was sure my package impressed her. For every time I flashed her, I would tell her my thing was four inches.

"I don't want to see no small ass four-inch ding-a-ling," Felesha said.

Not wanting to be out talked by a girl, I followed up with, "No girl, it's 4 inches from the ground."

She'd cover her mouth, eyes wide, and burst out laughing. Yeah... it was one of those smiles—you know, the kind which says, "I like what I see," a smile full of satisfaction.

I didn't exactly mind stripping down in front of her—Candy had already let it slip that Felesha was into that kind of thing. She had that heat in her eyes, that look that said she liked the chase as much as the catch. I used to get her running just so I could watch her curves move, that perfect rhythm in her stride like a Harlem Globetrotter dribbling down the court. Yeah... yeah, it's one of those dumb tricks teenage boys pull. Say what you want—it works.

There were times I'd chase her off, away from curious eyes, until she'd slow down and turn back toward me. It wasn't some movie scene with soft grass and golden light—no white-picket fantasy. We met in the alley, where trashcans leaned like old drunks and broken furniture waited to be forgotten. That's where she'd come close, lean in, and whisper things meant only for me.

"Can I grab it?"

And of course, my young ass response was, "Give me a kiss and your number first."

Now tell me—what kind of fool picks a kiss over a full-on grab? Yeah, that'd be me. Certified idiot. My mom always said I was a little slow on the uptake. Anyway, she reached down first, bold as ever, and I followed her lead, hands on her chest like I knew what I was doing. Felt like I was making moves, but that's as far as it went. Still, I got her number. And I'll say this: no fresh gear, no sharp fade, but I still walked away feeling like I'd won something. It was one of those wild nights made for kids and teenagers, the kind where the grownups were too busy chasing smoke to notice we were out till 4 a.m., writing our own stories in the dark.

At the end of the night Tucker, Candy, Felesha, myself, and some other kids were all sitting on Grandma Inas' front steps. With me trying to be cool with impressing the girls, I decided to take my little pranks a little further. Instead of dropping the trench coat and taking off streaking, I decided to fake like I had to use the bathroom in the house. I stood and walked to the top, and as I approached the top, I pulled out my little Minnie Me and started urinating over all their heads.

Honestly, I thought it was freaking hilarious, but they did not share in my humor. I thought they were all going to laugh, but instead, they did the exact opposite. The only one who found my stunt funny was Felesha. But maybe she was simply excited to see little Minnie Me again, who knows but her?

The night of my grand day did not go as well as it started. First, my home girl Candy went and told my father, but I could not blame her. Who would want a teenager squirting a golden shower on them? Of course, Levi came outside, still high as Hell and slapped me so hard, I heard the thunderclap.

I did all the work to impress Felesha, and all I got was getting put in place by my Old Man. What got to me was the fact Levi slapped the shit out of me in front of Felesha, but completely ignored the fact Tucker had bucked back at our mother and was getting away with it. Levi did not ask or pay any attention to why Tucker was around there all day. All he was focused was laying his monster of a hand upside my head. And by no means was my father fat or weak. In his late thirties, he was all bronze and muscle, muscles I am glad did not get laid on me worse than it had.

The Sunday after the block party on Stricker Street, Mother Sue came over to Grandma Laura's house and spoke to Mom about the fellow they called Jesus Christ. Not soon after Mom started going to church more often. I wasn't sure if Jesus Christ really walked with Mother Sue or if it was something meant to happen; either way, Mom began to change. Besides going to church more frequently, her visits to Grandma Inas on Stricker Street decreased, which I believe ended her drug use days. In the days which followed, all mom did was go to church and work.

Now, round on Stricker Street by eavesdropping, I found out the real reason Levi and Dennis did not return from their trip on time. While on their drug run up to New Jersey, Levi decided to taste their product some more while they were staying in a local hotel. Apparently, Levi had over-dosed on the white power. If it were not for his best friend Dennis and another guy they were with working to bring Levi back to life, I would have lost my father thirty plus years ago.

So, I posed the same question to myself again, what would my life have been like if my father was not around? All I could say is my family's life would have been drastically different. But Thank God somebody was praying for our father Levi Carter 3rd that day.

The day after the block party, everyone was getting ready to leave Grandma Ina's house since they had all stayed overnight. I said my goodbyes to my family and Felesha.

She whispered, "I better call her," and I ensured her I would.

I didn't let it show, but inside I was buzzing. Felesha was beautiful in a way that made my chest hum—I swear, I almost broke into song. But like every good weekend, the magic had to fade. I headed back to Grandma Laura's house, the place where Monday waited with schoolbooks and early alarms. *Ahh, the worries of a teenager.*

When school let out that Monday, I came home to find Tucker back with us. First thing I asked was what Levi had said or done to him. Tucker just shook his head—said he hadn't seen Levi since the night before. My mind went straight to the worst: maybe Levi was out chasing another hit, or maybe he was laid out somewhere, overdose written all over him. I looked at my little brother, standing there quiet, and I felt my chest sink. Just a week ago, we almost lost our father to cocaine. That kind of close call doesn't leave you—it lingers, like smoke in your lungs.

As the week went on we noticed we had not seen Levi since Sunday, and it was Thursday. We had grown accustomed to seeing our father every day, except when he went on his little business runs.

We asked Mom if she had spoken to Levi or seen him lately. She called all of us into the house and told us, "I don't want Y'all going around y'all Grandma's house while your father is not there."

"Where's Daddy at?" Nick asked. Nick was the only one to call Levi, Daddy and our mother, Mommy. The rest of us called our father by his first name, and we often called our mother 'Kay.'

"Remember I don't want Y'all around the corner until your father gets back home," she continued.

"Where is he?" Dominic asked again with a concerned voice.

Now I am flipping out on the inside because I know about the overdose. I was concerned he was going to die and before I could ask about it, Quick yelled out, "Can we see him?" as he was only asking what we were all thinking.

Kay explained to us how Levi went into a special hospital and that we cannot go and visit him because it was for adults only. I felt like saying, "What?" But I dare not say 'what' out loud to our mother, as I learned from Tucker's mistake of talking back. My mother is a genuine LADY, but when it came to butt whooping time, she did not play around, all games would be out the window.

To ease our little hearts, she said, "Y'all father is coming along well. He'll be calling me this evening. After I talk to him, I'll let Y'all speak to him."

And like a bunch of black Brady Bunch kids, we all responded simultaneously by saying, "YEAAAH."

As our mother looked at four happy faces, she said, "Y'all love your father don't you," with a smile of her own.

We all responded again as a group, "Yes."

Levi finally called around 7:00 pm and told us he was doing okay, adding his caretakers said he should be back home in 30 days. The first thing which came to mind was, *wow 30 days is a long time, and I need to call Candy and tell her about this.* After we all had spoken to our father, Mom got back on the phone to finish talking with him. Kay was on the phone with Levi for what felt like hours. At around 8:30 pm she got off the phone with him and sent us to take baths and go to bed, or as Grandma Laura always put it, "Draw the water and hit the bed."

The next day Raw and I walked to school, as we both went to Harlem Park Middle School. Harlem Park was a rough and tough school. It sat in the middle of three different neighborhoods which had their gangs: C.B.S, to Murphy Holmes Projects and E.A (Edmondson Avenue).4 These were the types of neighborhoods where you had to watch what you said, what you did, what you wore and who you looked at. You did any of those things wrong, and it could mean a very bad day for you.

All the rough kids, well let me say, it seemed as though all the rough kids in Baltimore went to Harlem Park. Harlem Park in the 80's was simply terrible. The school walls had graffiti on them; some lights were dim and flickered. They tried their hardest to keep the floors clean because the floors were the only clean thing in the entire building. And the lockers which did not have locks on them were filled with trash from top to bottom by the students. It kind of reminds you of the school called "Eastside High School," from the movie Lean On Me.

And I do not want to forget to tell you about the restrooms if you got caught slipping in the bathroom at the wrong time with another set of niggaz your ass was grass. Your ass would get jumped and be sent to the hospital. One day, there was a shootout in the main hallway entrance because someone tried to rob a dude for his Starter jacket. The crazy thing was both the dudes came to school with guns.

Was education worth losing our lives over? We as students did not give a fuck what happened at Harlem Park Middle School; we still went because we had heart, "Mutha Fucka!"

Harlem Park had four housing units; they were: Gilmore House, Calhoun House, Harlem House and Lafayette House. I was in Harlem House for my 6th and 7th-grade years. Raw was in Gilmore House for his 6th-grade year and before he spent his 7th and 8th-grade years in Harlem House. I was moved into the Calhoun House for my 8th-grade year, and 6th and 7th-grade years were smooth sailings in comparison. Once you got to Calhoun House, no one was about any foolishness. We were all in the 8th, and we couldn't wait for high school.

I had my little team or group I hung out with, my homeboys' names were John Blick, Rico Smith, Russell White, Obie Jones, and Mackenzie Danton. My dude Rico was from Baltimore Street. John was from the Murphy Holmes

Projects. And Russell, Obie, and McKenzie were all from the notorious C.B.S gang. Like my cousin Stan, they always had the freshest gear and looked sharp. Me, I'm looking normal enough to chill with the fellas. But unlike Stan, they were all little hardheaded kids who did not want to learn shit.

Out of the five of them, John was the only one who I clicked 5 with the most. I should have known this dude was about his business from the start, as he had tear drops on his face as an adolescent with more tattoos on his hands and arms.

We beat up girls or dudes; and if we caught you slipping, well you got your ass robbed. We robbed young bitches because they were the ones who tried to get you to their house for their click to rob you.

There were a few times we caught some young kids rolling dice in the restroom. Bad move. Hate to say it, but we left them laid out on that cold tile, blood smeared across the floor. I wasn't even built for that kind of violence—at least not until it came for me first.

Not too long later, it happened in that same restroom. Six dudes jumped me because one of them claimed the toilet I was using was "his." He stepped up like he owned the place, and I didn't hesitate—I swung first, put everything I had into it, and dropped him cold. But the rest of them? They tore into me, fists and feet flying, no mercy.

After that, something shifted. I started looking for payback, anyone I could catch in that restroom. Deep down, I was hoping I'd run into those same dudes again—with my crew behind me this time.

I did not fight as much in school as my homies did, but I figured people knew I was nothing to be played with. The main reason I did what was somewhat expected of me was because if I messed up, my parents would deliver their favorite disciplinary hobby. You guessed it, 'a whooping.' Yeah, I did my dirt in school. You know I could not be too soft if I wanted to survive. So, I did the basic things like play and joke around in class, fight here and there, flirt with the girls by feeling on their butts, squeezing their breast or the best flirting there was, rubbing on their privates when they wore dresses. I still was not having sex yet, but one thing was for sure. I did love the girls!

One day while the gang and I were sitting in class I noticed one of the other student's name was Johnny Johnson, and I thought, *man his name is familiar.*

Me being the talkative type asked the dude, "Do you know Mr. J.J or Johnny Johnson?"

"Yeah," he responded, "My pops name is Johnny Johnson, but he ran out on us years ago."

"That's weird," I continued, "Because my aunt married a man named Johnny Johnson. Where do you live?"

"On Mount Street off Laurence Street," he said.

I told him Raw, and I walked the same way home after school, so we could walk with him and talk more about the situation. I continued by telling him Raw was my cousin, he was over in Gilmore House, and I believed his father was most likely married to Raw's mother.

I quickly learned it was a small world, but today proved how small the world could be.

After talking it up for a few more minutes, he agreed to walk with us after school lets out.

By three o'clock, the school bells had done their job—day officially over. But what came next was a whole different scene. The area around Harlem Park Middle turned into a magnet for the neighborhood's hardheads. Every afternoon like clockwork, the gangs and street hustlers showed up, posted outside like it was their personal turf. The drug dealers were mostly older boys—ones who'd dropped out and decided the corner was their classroom now. And if it wasn't them hanging around, it was the glue sniffers, faces blank, eyes cloudy, chasing a high like it was all they had left. Yeah, you heard me correctly, *glue sniffers.*

Glue sniffers were a whole different breed. They'd rip cotton from old mattresses or grab a handful of balls, soak it in Kwicky or paint thinner, then squeeze it into a tight little wad that fit right in their palm. All day long, they'd hold it to their nose, breathing in those toxic fumes like it was oxygen. I don't know who came up with that dumb-ass idea, but every afternoon, you'd see at least fifty of them posted up around the school, zoned out and chasing that high. Me? I wanted more. I wanted the finer things—the fast cash, the fresh kicks, the respect the drug dealers had. But I knew better. Pops would've buried me if he found out I was even thinking about slinging. That kind of life came with a price I wasn't ready to pay.

Now ask yourself, how does this make for a good scene or educational environment every single damn day? If it is not violent people hanging around on the school property, it was high as hell violent people hanging on school property.

Fights between rival gangs became a regular thing—sometimes over turf, sometimes just because one crew caught a lone member slipping. Didn't take much to spark it. By the time the final bell rang at Harlem Park Middle, school and city cops were already posted up, trying to keep the chaos from spilling over. But on this particular day, it was different. The authorities must've been locked in, because the gangs kept it cool. No fights broke out. Still, the energy was thick—loud voices, side-eyes, and that kind of movement that made you feel like something could pop off any second

Through all the noise, people, and confusion happening outside I found Raw and introduced him to my classmate Johnny, last name Johnson. And believe me I made sure to enunciate, emphasize, and separate his first and last name so Raw would get my point. On the walk home, the three of us learned a lot about one another. I even shared my father's situation with them. I told them Levi was in the hospital for thirty days. And Raw being Mr. Intelligent wanted to know the details, so I filled him in. I explained I had learned this from talking to my father on the phone the day before.

Raw joking around like he normally did, saying, "Levi probably in the rehab," but he quickly followed with, "Sike boy, I'm joking."

We all laughed at the joke, but it did ring a bell in my mind. I started thinking back on the grown folks' conversation about Levi's overdose. I would have told Raw about Levi's overdose, but Johnny was with us, so I let it go.

The school was about five city blocks away from Grandma Laura's house and maybe eight or so blocks from Johnny's house. After talking about Levi, I got quiet and let Raw and Johnny's talk about their parental situation as I pondered on my dilemma and spent a few of those minute's thinking about Felesha. With my mind focused on elsewhere, we covered those city blocks in no time.

When we got to Winchester Street, Mr. J.J and my Aunt Evelyn happened to be pulling up in their car. They both waved when they saw us, but I am not sure if Mr. J.J even knew who Johnny was at the time. But with the expression on Johnny's face, I was certain he knew who Mr. J.J was. I had to break the tension as we walked over to them.

"Hey Mr. J.J do you know this dude," I asked.

"Son is that you?" He asked after a double take and squinting of the eyes, trying to make out the familiar face.

I was not sure how I felt about the situation, as Johnny looked both happy and sad at the same time. As I walked away to speak to Grandma Laura, they continued to exchange hugs and talked for a little longer. I could only imagine how Johnny felt, knowing his father left him and his family to be with another woman—and to seem very happy as well.

Once in the house and before I had the opportunity to speak to Grandma, she said, "Boy, please call your cousin Candy. She's been ringing my phone like there is no tomorrow, calling four times in fifteen minutes."

"Ok Grandma," I said with a smile. *Man, she one crazy old lady.*

With the phone in hand, I called Candy back and of course the first thing she said to me was, "Yo, you know your father is in rehab?"

I was close to saying something ignorant back to her, but she quickly cut my thoughts off saying, "Levi almost died in New Jersey when they left that weekend."

I was like *Whoa!* I remembered Raw saying something earlier about my father being in rehab and I wondered if he knew more than what he was putting on at the time. The song *Dopeman* by N.W.A 7 instantly popped into my head, as the lyrics spoke about the drug game and fiends asking the dope man for another hit. And I could not help but ask and wonder to myself, was my father a drug addict? Was he going to end up like the addicts I see on the streets begging and asking for money? Knowing this, my mind started to run a thousand miles a minute.

My mind drifted, then snapped back to that moment—Candy whispering all the things Felesha liked, painting the picture clear. And then, like a spark in the dark, Felesha's voice talking in the background, playful and low, her

32

words curling around me: "Ooh Will... Ooh Will, please do it harder." That memory didn't just linger—it pulsed.

In a flash, my thoughts veered from memories of my father to the way Felesha had begged for more—her voice echoing in my head, urgent and breathless. I told Candy to hand her the phone. When Felesha came on, we slipped into conversation, voices low and charged, until my grandmother suddenly picked up the line, saying she needed to make a call. And honestly, I was a little embarrassed when Felesha ended our conversation saying, "Oh you gotta get off the phone little boy," in her seductive voice again.

I could not help but wonder where she was getting all this stuff from, but I quickly put those thoughts aside as I responded by saying, "I got your little boy right here," she laughed, and we said our good-bye's, not knowing it was going to be our last time talking. Not too long after this conversation Felesha got pregnant at the age of fourteen by some drug dealer in her neighborhood.

After finishing my last conversation with Felesha, I told my grandmother, I was off the phone, and I went back outside where I found Mr. J.J and Johnny talking. I thought to myself, how can a man not be in contact with his child for these many years? I vowed to myself if I ever had a child I would be there for them whenever they needed me! I reflected on my life, realizing my father was there every day of my life except for now. I remember feeling a deep emptiness inside, thinking this was the moment I wanted and needed my father the most.

CHAPTER FOUR: THE CHOICES

The summer of 1988 is here, and Grandma Inas brought all her grandkids who graduated from the 8th grade a gold tooth. Man, a good summer it was turning out to be. I graduated to the 9th grade, I got me a gold tooth, and my father was back home with us. To me, it appeared the events of my father nearly overdosing woke him up, as now Levi was even more active with us and was going to church with my mother. And nearly every Sunday, he would gather the family together, and we would go as a family with him to Mother Sue's church.

In the past few weeks and months, it appeared the Lord had been working on my family and all its problems. For the Lord had redeemed my father, and now our parents were announcing we were moving into our house on Appleton Street. As a family, I never saw us so excited before, and we showed every ounce of excitement that day.

One Sunday in church when my father did not attend, my mother sung this song called *Precious Lord*. And to say she sung it would be an understatement— Kayden Hill blew it out of the water! Looking at her as she stood at the foot of the pulpit, I could not help but think and know the Lord had complete control over my mom's life. You may know this song, but I still could not help but include a few Lyrics:

Precious Lord, take my hand, Lead me on. Let me stand. I am tired, I am weak, I am worn. Through the storm, through the night. Lead me on, to the Light. Take my hand Precious Lord and Lead me home!

When she finished singing, she received a standing ovation from every church member, and although I was not so in touch with my religious side, I was touched by it. Right then and there, I knew the Lord was present in my mother's life. Where did Kay get the courage to sing in front of a full church like she did? I swear, within a month the whole family was in church to join her. Grandma Inas, Uncle Melvin, Aunt Faith, and Regina. Valencia brought Candy and her little sister Lisa to my mother's church. Seeing this I learned prayer worked because I did not see this coming in a million years, I never thought I would see my crazy family going to church.

We finally moved from Winchester Street and out of Grandma Laura's house into our house on Appleton Street in July of 1988. My father was working for this company named C.A.C or Circular Advertisement Company. My father must have been a good worker because management allowed him to use the company truck to move his family.

After packing the truck and pulling off, we arrived at **The Hole** several minutes later. **The Hole** is what we came to call the 1100 block of North Appleton Street, giving it the name because it was only one block with one way in and one way out, a dead-end block. It ended with at a pair of operating train tracks which was blocked off by a ten-foot fence. It was the perfect place to raise a family of all boys as the dead end lessened the amount of traffic flow on the street.

We moved into the three-bedroom brick row home with one bathroom in the rear of the second floor, living room, dining room, kitchen, and basement. It was nothing grand, but it was something we could call home.

When we pulled up, my father jumped out of the truck to come around and open up the rear door to the truck to let us out. Raising the truck door, we all leaped out with no shirts or shoes on. We were what you might call 'Straight Hood Vikings!' We started moving furniture into the house as the people in the block sat on their fronts and watched us like we were crazy. They were probably asking themselves, *who in the world moves wearing no shirts or shoes?*

Man, I cannot emphasize how many pretty girls were out and with every last one of them right for the taking. Well, not really good for the taking. Their ruff neck boyfriends stood back watching their women, looking like they were ready to start trouble if we attempted to talk to them. We did not know the neighbors next door on our left but come to find out in the days which followed they were our first cousins. I was glad to see we had family in a totally new neighborhood. I did already know one and his name was Travis.

I knew Travis from him working on the A-rab horse and wagons always strolling through many of the neighborhoods. He often came through Stricker Street with a wagon full of fruit—apples, plums, peaches, watermelons, cantaloupe, grapes, strawberries, and more. If you named it, he probably had it. And all this time I never knew he was my kinfolk.

Why do they call it A-rabbing? I am not sure; maybe it was similar to caravan trading in the Middle East or something?

Anyway, we moved into 1109 Appleton Street in the summer of 1988. But the Lord did not stop working in our family because on October 2, 1988, a day before me and my father's birthday, our parents Levi and Kayden got married at Temple Christ Baptist Church. And it was Mother Sue's husband Reverend Odenton who married them.

It amazes me how some people seemed to be made for each other and how they could love one person for the remainder of their lives. How about Levi and Kayden? Some people can hold it together; how about us? And this little tune comes to mind when writing about Levi and Kayden......*My Father came a long way to become the man he is today. To top everything off my mother's last name is our last name, Carter.*

My father came a long way to become the man he was on their wedding day. All the cocaine sniffing, reefer smoking, and beer drinking Levi had become accustomed to no longer existed. He was always a great guy in my eye, but it was something about this man now which made me love him much more. And like I said, the entire family started coming to church. My Aunt Faith—the one who beat Tucker—started coming to church so often, I could hardly believe it. She had stopped smoking cigarettes, and even put the weed down. Church became a must in my family.

Sometimes I sit and think to myself, thinking if it were not for Faith beating Tucker up the way she did the family would still be the same as we were. If it were not for Levi telling my mother to take us around the corner on Winchester Street to live with Grandma Laura, the family would most likely still be on drugs. If it were not for Grandma Laura introducing Mother Sue to my Mother

Kayden (a.k.a Kay), the family would still be a mess. If it were not for Levi overdosing in New Jersey and Dennis helping to revive him to life, the family would still believe God was not real. Do you see where I am going with this? The truth is Jesus Christ is real, and I truly believe everything happened for a reason.

I trust and believe if my father never went to rehab, he would still be out in the world doing his own thing. Sometimes, even the bad things have to happen, so we find a reason to call on God and believe. After he had found God, my father would get up every Sunday morning and go around picking up everyone who did not have transportation to church. Can you say *dedication*?

I enjoyed going to church to hear Rev. Odenton preach, even at my young age. I referred to Rev. Odenton's preaching as *Fly Gospel Fly*. Rev. Odenton was eighty-three years old, and it was usually hard for him to get around. But when it came to him preaching and delivering his sermon, let me tell you, this eighty-three-year-old man would jump up off the pulpit like he had wings. There were times Rev. Odenton ran around the small church so fast, it was hard to believe he had any problems with his legs. *Fly Gospel Fly* was his message.

I cannot tell you exactly what the message was about because it was so long ago, but the part I do remember is his excitement and enthusiasm for delivering God's word.

Not long after marrying my mother and father, Rev. Odenton passed away from cancer. It makes me wonder if he was referring to himself and his departure from this earth when he was preaching *Fly Gospel Fly* or was, he simply giving a word.

I was shocked when I learned he had died. I loved Rev. Odenton like he was my grandpa, and I believed the rest of the family saw him the same way, as they all came to attend the funeral. Reverend Odenton's funeral was the first funeral I ever attended, and he was the first dead person I ever saw. I think seeing a dead person did something to me that day, because to this day I struggle with being around them or the idea of being around them.

So, did the Lord keep Reverend Odenton here on earth long enough to marry my parents? I do not know. But I would like to think so!

««« ♠♠ »»»

A few months later and it's the end of the year for 1988. We're living in a new house and honestly it felt like we were a family again. The relatives next door turned out to be good people and we became close to them almost immediately. Maybe there is some truth to the saying, *blood is thicker than water.*

We had five older cousins next door; they were Davis, Mitch, Janice, Charles, and Smiley. Next came the three younger cousins Destiny, Emmanuel, and LaQuin but people know him as Tittie City. They were all brothers and sisters; their mother was Aunt Barbara or Mrs. B. as some people came to call her.

Appleton Street was what my family needed, as our close-knit family became even closer. Although Appleton Street was a dead end, it was not dead by any means. Everybody came around to our block because something was always happening, and that's not in a negative sense. The different families in this block came to act as one large family block which looked out for one another by any means.

However, simply because we acted as a family block, does not mean we were living in *Green Acres.* We still lived within the boundaries of Baltimore City, and with the city came the older guys who stood on the corners, either drinking, selling drugs or next in line to become gang bangers. All city corners are the same, no matter what angle you look from.

One day when I was walking home from school, I happened to come up on this fight going down on my block. This little guy was stomping all the crap out this other dude. These dudes were getting it in. As everybody came out to watch the fight, I noticed my homey from Harlem Park run up to the fight as if he knew what was going on. When it came to this gangsta shit I had no doubt about my abilities to get down, so I walked up, "Yo J.?" I called out to John, but he was trying to break up the fight as the police were on their way.

Since Western District was only four blocks away, the police could get to us in no time. But if you were to stand on the corners of Appleton and Riggs, you would be able to see the police coming down from over the hill where the police station was located. By the time the police got to the spot where the fighting was taking place, everybody had already cleared the scene.

"Yo Will," John shouted back as he waved me over. Stepping beside him I quickly gave him a dap, and he introduced me to the dude doing the stomping. "Hey, Will this is my cousin Midget." Midget and I locked eyes and shook hands. Had I known at the time what I know now, I would've realized I was shaking hands with a true lifelong friend.

"Y'all just moved around in **The Hole**," asked Midget as he started talking with his hands like you see in those Italian mafia movies.

"Hell yeah. And I didn't know you're crazy ass was my homey cousin," I responded, taking on a tougher posture than normal.

"Yeah, what can I say, Test is my cousin," Midget continued looking over at John. John laughed with an expression which said, *FUCK YEAH. THAT'S MY NAME.* From this moment on I never called him John again, as he would ride and die with the name Test.

Midget was brown skinned with a small mole under his eye, but what tripped me out the most was his bald head. The only people I ever saw with them were old white cops.

After our brief introduction on the corner of Riggs and Appleton, the two of them took me around into one of the alleys where a gang of rough-looking dudes was fixing bikes in their backyards.

"Will I want you to meet Midget's brother Nelson, our partners Rue, Corey and K'mar," Test introduced. And when I say rough, I do not mean dirty by any means. I am talking about an aura stating we are not to be played with. In all honesty, they may have been rough, but I quickly came to learn in the weeks to come they were ordinary teenagers like me.

Nelson was tall, with a deep dark complexion and a scar on his chin he got from a bike fall. Rue was fair skinned and what we referred to as a pretty boy. Corey was short, had a high-top fade with parts in his eyebrow like Big Daddy Kane. Finally, there was K'mar; he was obviously the strongest of them all based on his cocky ass arms, fair skinned with a lazy right eye.

"Wud up my niggaz," was all I had to say for this was no formal greeting. This marked a turning point in my life. From this moment on I never went without friends again. I now had people to hang with other than my little brothers.

Looking in the yard, these boys had tools everywhere, grip pliers, needle nose pliers, screwdrivers, pipe wrenches (which we also called monkey wrenches), hammers, etc. The yard was the equivalent of an auto body shop but for bikes as the yard was littered with random bike parts.

At one point Nelson yelled up the alley to his little brother Gary who was walking past. When Gary came to see what his big brother wanted, I see my little brother Dominic right with him. I'm like, *Whoa!* We squadding up!

"Hey, Dominic how do you know Lil Gary," I asked.

"We met while playing Hide and Go Seek," he responded.

However, we often played Hide and Seek a little different than most kids. Often calling it Hide and Go Freak, as we would try our best to get some of the neighborhood girls as our hiding partner. And this was when the real fun began.

Both Gary and Dominic went running back up the alley, looking nothing short of two orphan kids. Nelson had sent Gary to the store to buy him some patches and glue. Now patches and glue cost about $2 for a box, but they were a must have if you intended to fix a flat on a bike tire, something I learned how to do years ago when living on Winchester Street.

At the beginning of the summer of 1989, I graduated from the 8th grade and the following year I would be attending Walbrook Senior High School located in Walbrook Junction. I heard so much about High School and knowing about it made me so anxious because I had my team and they said the young ladies in the school were off the hook.

My older cousins next door to me filled me in with just about everything concerning The Brook. When I finally got up in the school, I was trippin because it was actually two schools put together. The actual building sat in The Junction directly behind the shopping center. Unfortunately, we could not immediately use the building because of asbestos. Opening day was delayed because of asbestos removal, and the entire school was merged with Southwestern High School in Southwest Baltimore until the removal was complete. And the combining of these two schools meant nothing but trouble.

Exactly as I expected, I got into a fight on the first day of school over some dude's girl I wasn't even messing with. This dude named Jake from Southwestern pops the shit out me while I was in the cafeteria, thinking I was someone else! I did not give a fuck who he thought or what he thought; he hit the wrong guy today.

Afterward, we got along fine. He got sent to the office because he did not belong in the café when Walbrook was in there anyway. I didn't hang with my round-the-way homies at all during school. In fact, I didn't even see them the entire day.

I thought to myself; *I'll have to fucking kill one of them whores' next time. I can't believe this shit happened on the first day of school.* In the process of fighting, I messed up my brand-new pair of Reebok Classic's, the all-white ones with the gray trimming, knowing damn well I have to take care of what name brands I have. I do not know what genius thought it was a good idea to put these two rival schools together. For I had seen at least two fights today alone.

But that was not the end to my first day. Once I got home from school, I happened to find the front door leaning against the front of the house, completely off its hinges. Walking into the house, I promptly asked my brothers what in the world was going on? For some reason, my little brother Nick always knew everything going on. Even when he wasn't there, he could recite events with deadly accuracy — a trait my father eventually came to love.

Nick quickly told me some boys had chased Tucker home from school. So I went straight to Tucker to hear his side of the story and find out what it had to do with the front door.

Tucker explained how he was chased home from school and when he got home the door was locked, so he knocked it down. Although I was mad my brother got chased home from school, I was even more upset he kicked down the door. I could not help but think to myself, *what type of shit is this? Isn't the door locked every day you come home from school? Isn't this why they call it a door?* My next thoughts went to my father, as Levi did not play any jokes, no questions asked he was going to knock our blocks off!

I tried to push the impending concerns of Levi aside and attempted to focus on who had chased my brother home from school? However, it didn't work either—my mind kept going back to the fucking door, off its fucking hinges, and how my fucking parents were on their fucking way home, no doubt ready to beat our fucking asses! Why? Because of my fucking brother's dumb ass fucking decision.

I got so fucking frustrated thinking about the ass whooping coming my way, I popped Tucker without a shred of remorse for what he had been through. I knew his school Calverton Middle School was a good distance away and how he had to walk through rival neighborhoods to get to school, well in his case run home from school. But kicking the door off the hinges was no excuse! *What, they chased his ass all the way to the front door or some shit?*

It was like old times again with me and Tucker fighting, and we fought until our parents came home. Our father walked into the house, asked not one question and simply started throwing his blows. No need to unlock a door, right? Why, because it was sitting on the front.

Remember I told you my father was no small guy, and now, being grown, he packed even more of a punch—punches I couldn't handle. Once he popped me a couple of times, I turned to my last resort and pretended to faint. Yeah, a *Bitch* move right? But you have to see it. My eyes saw two fish the size of sledgehammers pummeling me.

From the moment on, whenever he started throwing blows, I fainted, which more often than not saved me from multiple ass whoopings. It got to the point my parents even started taking me to the hospital because they thought my father had injured me somehow. But this wasn't the case; it was simply some good ass acting on my part. I know not to get back up after a grown man like my father causes your chest to greet your back.

Tucker, on the other hand, did not know the meaning of tapping out. Every time he was punched, he would swell up and poke his chest out like he did to my mother a few years back. Unlike with my mother, Tucker knew not to swing back on Levi. If Tucker had ever thrown a punch at Levi, his life would have most likely ended.

All jokes aside! My father simply did not play games. When I tell you Levi went ape shit on Tucker, he beat Tucker like he was a nigga on the street. He was so in tune to whooping Tucker's ass he forgot about the front door being off the hinges until our mother came up screaming at Dominic and Quick about the front door.

She came in like a heat-seeking missile—no hesitation, no questions—just straight fury. Quick and Nick didn't stand a chance as she started beating the brakes off them. In the middle of the madness, Tucker was hollering about getting chased home from school by a pack of boys. That day? Pure chaos. Our house was a war zone. With two adults and four kids, meant nothing but Ass Whooping Mania. Nearly thirty minutes into Ass Whooping Mania, Levi finally delivered his last blow to Tucker's ribs. After this incident, we had to stay in and go to bed by 6:00 pm every night until our parents finally eased up—which was long after.

Days after the door incident when I would go to school, my neighborhood friends would ask why we do not come outside anymore? I had to explain the entire story—how Tucker got chased home, how he and I started fighting, how my father came home and caught us, and finally, how Tucker tried to swell up on Levi but got beat down. I often tried to make the story funny so they wouldn't think our family belonged in an insane asylum or something similar, saying things like how my cousin next door could hear the belt whistle through the air. They always got a good laugh out of that, but the truth was, the real thing was not as funny as it seemed. Levi's fists were not to be played with. One would think we would learn a lesson from all of them monsoon-like whoopings but let the truth be told.... we did not.

When our parents were at work, we would have our friends over the house. We knew exactly what time our parents got home, so we planned around it. One day, however, Levi came home early, and we heard him pull up in the car. I believe Levi & Kay had one of those 1993 Brown Chevrolet Caprice Station Wagons, with a 5.7L V-8. Yo, this bitch was so damn loud because it needed a muffler. Shorty, the car's front bumper was falling off, so my father tied it up with some clothesline rope. It was a tacky ass job, but the car never broke down on him—at least, I never heard of it happening.

Now we were not supposed to have company in the house when our parents were not home. But on this day, like any other day, we did not listen and had a house full of friends, when someone heard my parent's station wagon entering onto the block. We immediately put everybody in the house out the back door. We pulled the wool over Levi's eyes that day; he thought he was going to catch us with our hands in the cookie jar.

Little did we know, when we thought we got over on Levi, Aunt B. next door informed our father about us having a little gathering in the house while they were at work. Levi did not hesitate to come into the house and let us have it again. I was in the 9th grade and was still getting my ass whooped like a three-year-old! Quick and I simply took our whooping and got it out of the way. Dominic was still too young, so he was safe....at the moment. As for Tucker, he was another story.

Like every other time Levi popped Tucker, he stood there as if it didn't affect him. Levi grabbed Tucker by his left arm, raised it up in the air and socked my brother so hard in the ribs I thought I heard them crack. Tucker had no choice but to go down hard! Why couldn't my brother simply take it like Quick and I? After the beating, I wanted to call the police and report our suspicion of fatherly abuse. The only reason I didn't call them was because of my fear they might release Levi for good behavior, and I was too afraid to take the chance. Yo, Levi was straight up crazy or was he back on some shit again?

On New Years of 1990, our parents went out and left me in charge of the house. I was not in charge because we still had Aunt B next door spying on us. Later in the night, our big cousins Charles, David, and Mitch headed out back and fired their guns in the air to bring in the New Year.

To ring in the New Year, Tucker and Quick kicked things off by hurling eggs at each other—right there in the house. No matter how hard or how often our father laid into us, we only seemed to get wilder. I joined the madness, grabbed a jar of jelly from the fridge, and launched it at Quick. That was all it took. We were deep into a full-blown food fight. Poor Nick just stood there, wide-eyed, watching us act a fool.

Maybe he was taking notes on what not to do. He might've tossed one egg, maybe two, but whatever damage he did couldn't hold a candle to the destruction Tucker, Quick, and I unleashed. By the time we were done, egg yolk and jelly coated everything—the floors, the ceiling, the walls. Nothing was safe. It was glorious, stupid chaos.

Eventually, one of our big cousins from next door came to check on us. When he knocked on the door, it scared all the crap out of me. It suddenly dawned on me Kay and Levi might be standing on the other side. Now remember, we have not been outside to play with our friends since the summer of 1989. You might think we would have learned a lesson by now. Nooo Way! Now I was standing on the other side of the door scared as hell. With every second there was another knock on the door.

"Who is it," I asked.

"It's your cousin Travis punk! Open this door coon," he replied. I opened the door shaking in my boots thinking it was Levi.

"What's up," I asked Travis, not wanting him to see the mess we made inside the house from our little food fight.

"Will I come to see if you wanted to Bang off this .44 magnum for the New Year."

With me being 15, having my big cousin come over and ask me if I wanted to shoot some guns was like giving me a million dollars. I jumped on the opportunity, "Ok.... Ok," I responded eagerly. One thing was for sure, and that was Levi would never put a gun in my hand at this age. Leaving out the house to go next door, I turned to my brothers, "Hey clean up the house before Levi and Kayden get home while I go next door with Travis for a little."

I thought we were going to go around in the back yard to shoot the guns like most people do every year in the city. But instead, my crazy cousin came out to the front of the house and started shooting. He was letting the trigger fly, *Bang.... Bang.*

With each shot my adrenaline increased with anticipation, "Travis let me hold it," I said as though I knew what I was doing. Instead of giving me the .44 magnum as he said, he gave me a 12-gauge shotgun.

WOOOW! Gripping the big ass gun felt awkward, mostly due to the anxiety I felt simply thinking about firing it. I knew shotguns had a huge kick to them, but I played it all off, and if you saw me, you would have thought I did this before.

I took hold of the cold steel and aimed it at the streetlight on the other side of the street and pulled the trigger. *BOOM!* My cousin Charles, Travis' brother, came out the house, "Travis you dumb ass. Take the gun from him before he kills somebody. Most likely himself!"

By this time, I was already amped up. My little brothers were now standing in the doorway watching me do my thing. While giving the gun back to Travis, I hear another gun go off. *BOOM! POP! POP! BOOM! POP!*

"Happy New Years," my older cousin Mitch yelled as he was shooting from the upstairs bedroom window.

BOOM! BOOM! BOOM! BOOM! POP! POP! POP! BOOM!

Was all you could hear for the next hour. You'd think the police would have shown up by now with all the gunplay going on. It got to the point where other neighbors came out of their houses, shooting, drinking, smoking reefer, and screaming, 'Happy New Years Mutha Fucka's!' It was like nothing I had ever experience before, as the neighborhood celebrated the New Year together illegally.

Good Times, I thought to myself. Amid all the controlled chaos, I had to go back and check on my brothers, making sure they had at least started cleaning up after the earlier food fight.

A quick check of the house showed everything was fine, so feeling the celebration vibe, I told my brothers to put on their coats and join our cousins outside for some fun. I was so eager to get back outside that I didn't notice the jelly and eggs running down the side of the living room wall.

Back outside the sky was set ablaze with the flashes of guns firing off into the night. And not only from our neighborhood but the surrounding neighborhoods, as you could hear guns being fired in the distance. My older cousins were so wild they even allowed their younger sister Destiny to shoot as well. They weren't so reckless as to let her shoot it on her own. Travis held her close as she shot the automatic 9mm. Once she pulled the trigger, she emptied around thirteen to seventeen rounds.

That's when I see my homeboy Test come out the alley saying, "Y'all round here setting it off," holding his hands up in the air as if he was making the letter 'Y' with his arms. "Damn Mr. Carter must be feeling good to let Y'all asses out of the house finally," he continued, going into his jacket to pull out a Mack-11.

"What's that I ask," I asked.

"This here is a mutha fuckin Mack-11 young man," he responded, aiming it to the sky. *Click! Click!* "Damn the bitch jammed," taking nearly twenty seconds he unjammed it, walking into the middle of the street with the Mack-11 aimed at the sky he latched onto the trigger. *La-la-la-la-la-la-la*, the Mack-11 ranged to life. And after what seemed like forever, the Mack-11 spent its magazine.

"Yo, Test! How many rounds it hold?" I asked.

"Fifty, but there's always one in the chamber," he replied.

I am telling you; his gun must have been the final straw or was enough to scare the folks in the block because they all came to the doors complaining, fussing, cursing and saying all old folks' favorite line, *'This don't make any damn sense.'* Test ran back into the alley once all the old people came out yelling.

One of Nick's little friends lived across the street named Cruddy came out. Now why they call this little ass boy Cruddy, I do not know, but can I say he was my brother's homeboy. I made a mental note to find out how he earned the name. I'd put my last dollar on him trying to be an up-and-coming gangsta, but not quite there yet. He went over and gave Nick a dap.

"Where is Levi?" My little Cousin Emmanuel asked from next door. Everybody knew my Pops was not wrapped too tight!

"Levi went out for the New Year," I answered. "Hey, Cousin David, what time is it?"

"2:37 am," he responded.

At this point I was thinking, *where are my parents?* While I was thinking, Nick yelled out, "Aunt B did Mommy or Daddy call?"

"Yeah, they called, and they should be on their way home by now. Is the house straight," she asked?

Tucker and Quick both looked at each other before they responded with a "Yes."

By this time in the morning all the guns had been put back up and secured, as my older cousins knew how the older folks were close to calling the cops. Everyone started sitting on their steps, and trash talked to one another about who let off the most shots or who had the prettiest gun.

Out of nowhere the police turned onto the 1000 block of Appleton Street and flew up the block, their destination the 1100 block of Appleton Street, my block, **The Hole**. Moments later, the helicopter was flashing its spotlight down into the block. One would think it was South Central because of how deep the police came. These cops had to be S.W.A.T or some gun squad, as they came with five cars, with four in each car. If you were outside at the time they searched you down for guns, no questions asked.

With all the lights and flashes in **The Hole**, I looked up and saw my mother running down the street towards us. I knew she was thinking to herself, *what the hell my boys do now?* She was immediately stopped by the police before she was able to reach us. They let her know they were checking everyone outside on the block for guns because of all the calls about gunshots.

Once she saw us standing on the steps safe, she calmed down. After about ten to fifteen minutes the police left, but not before stating, "This party is over folks. And if we have to come back, believe me, someone is getting locked up...."

Levi pulled in front of the house as soon as the police left. He had to wait until all the police left to free up some parking spaces. From the look on their faces, you could tell my parents had a long night. Afterwards, they spoke to everyone, and simply wished everyone a Happy New Year before calling it a night.

The following day on January 2, 1990, neither my brothers nor I had been outside for recreation or hung with our friends in five months. My Pops must have had a good night because he got up the next morning and told all of us to put clothes on so we could play basketball. We did not care about how cold it was outside, we just wanted to get out and be normal kids, you know? Or normal kids to the best of our ability.

It was close to noon by the time we all woke up, ate, and were dressed to leave. My parents had recently purchased this turquoise Toyota van could seat nine people easily. Levi circled the block loading up our neighborhood friends. He pulled up to Midget's house and grabbed him and his little brother Gary.

Looking at Gary, Levi stuttered the words, "Me dee me dee me wanna go," joking with him, as Gary always asked my father if he could go with us places. Packed in the Toyota van was my father, Tucker, Quick, Dominic, Gary, Nelson, Midget, Lil Cruddy, K'mar and me.

As Levi started to pull off, my two older friends lived next door to Nelson and Midget named Toll and Taylor asked if they could join us. When it came to balling and having a good game, Levi was all about it. Without hesitation, Levi yelled back to us in the van, "Make some room, because we have two more getting in." No matter how much Levi beat and punished us, he often took us out with him.

My brothers and I were only familiar with the basketball courts around our old way called *McKabee's* located near Gilmore and Laurence Street. But this day, Levi had filled up the gas tank and headed for the highway. We all looked around at each other trying to figure out where in the world he was taking us.

Hearing the whispering, Levi yelled out, "We going to B.W.I, near the airport to play with the white boys."

We instantly became pumped! I for one was most definitely pumped; I was finally out of the house and hanging with my closest friends in the New Year. When life seemed to get tough for my brothers and me, the simplest things always came around to make it enjoyable again.

It took us close to twenty minutes to get out to Glen Burnie and near the airport. Before reaching the courts, Levi stopped and brought lunch meat and snacks for all of us so we could have something to eat while gaming. Stepping onto the court, we found a couple of white boys shooting around. Come to find out they were his boss' sons.

Levi simply called them the Flecho's: they were Ronald, Gregory, and

Derrick and they also had a few of their friends on the court shooting around with them. When the game began, it was us against them, and even though it looked like black versus white, the reality was completely different. On this day, color was neither an issue nor a factor. It was all about the game.

Man, I do not know how we did it. We played basketball for about seven hours straight and nearly non-stop. We might have played longer if we had longer days of sunlight. Although the court had automatic lights, we didn't stay because Levi had to take everyone home. Those white boys beat us four games to our three games, but all in all, we still had fun. After eating the leftover lunchmeat sandwiches, Levi dropped everyone home by 8:00 pm.

When we got home and as soon as we walked in the house Kay yelled, "Who was throwing food in the house?" We all stopped in our tracks and remained silent. "There are eggs and jelly all up on the wall in the living room," she continued as Levi was coming through the front door, Kayden getting louder with each word she spoke. And with each one of Levi's steps, I was only thinking after a good day; *I have to come back to this.* Only one thing was going to come out of this....

"What happened, babe?" Levi asked my mother.

"Ask them?" she replied gesturing toward us with her hand out.

I guess with me being the oldest; he looked right at me with an emotionless stare, a stare I would never forget. Levi's face warned if you lied, it would be the end of your existence. It was a look I had seen before; it sure was not a good look then, and sure enough, it was not one at the moment.

"Levi, what happened?" he asked me.

"There is food on the living room walls," I mumbled under my breath.

"WHAT!" He yelled, stepping around us to look at our artistic food painting. "I bet you guys, neither one of you know what happened do Y'all?"

All four of us looked at him without saying a word, as there were no words to explain. What could we say, 'Oh we got bored and decided to throw eggs and jelly to amuse ourselves.' I doubt saying this would have appeased our situation.

"Since no one knows anything, take y'all clothes off." We all knew what was coming after those famous words, and with them, everyone started crying.

Man, I did not see what was coming next. As I was taking my clothes off, Levi slapped the shit out of me, knocking me to the floor. With me on the floor, Levi went to the next, who happened to be Nick. Looking into Nick's eyes, he asked, "What happened?" Before Nick could get a word out Levi punched little Nick in his stomach, Tucker and Quick would be next.

On the floor, I wondered, *how could he be so nice but so got damn mean and cruel at the same time?* Before I could come back to thought, I heard Nick telling on all of us. Levi had to slap Nick to get him to talk and had to slap him again to shut up.

Taking his belt off with his left hand, being he was left-handed, he replied, "OOOH! Y'all want to have a food fight with food I went out here and worked hard for huh? Put your hand out," he said, looking at Tucker, but instead of hitting his hands, he smacked Tucker across the top of his head with the thick leather belt. Instantly reacting to the pain, Tucker began jumping around holding his head. After hitting Tucker, in one smooth motion, he punched Quick in the mouth with the other hand.

He beat Nick for not telling. He beat me because I should have known better. He beat Quick because he was always getting into something. When he got back to Tucker again, he noticed he had knocked everything over from jumping around.

"Oh, so you wanna act dumb," Levi asked Tucker who remained silent but simply stuck out his chest again on Levi. "Why is it every time I pop you, you want to act like you big? If you're big like you think you are, fight me back." It was a sad day, for Levi beat Tucker for Damn near an hour. He would not have stopped if it was not for our mother telling him to.

After our daily routine of ass whooping, we were back to the grind of eating, and going straight to bed. No more outside for us at the moment. Huh, they must have forgotten we were still punished since August of '89'.

While at the table eating, Tucker continued to huff and puff, so Levi told Tucker he's not eating at the table with us. After that, he wrapped a belt around Tucker's neck and set his food in the corner. I could not believe what the hell I was witnessing. He told Tucker since he wants to sound and act like a dog, he has to eat like one. Which meant eating without using his hands, only his mouth. Now I had truly seen it all, and the idea of killing my father for this abuse flashed through my mind. *Our father does not love us* I thought. For the rest of the night, Levi made Tucker crawl around the house with the belt around his neck like a damn dog. My mother said whatever we got we deserved every bit of the punishment.

1109 Appleton Street had simply become HELL!

We haven't been out to play with our friends since Levi beat us back in January. We have been on punishment for eight months now. And it seems like the more we got punished, the more trouble we got into. I guess we figured we had nothing to lose.

There was this one time I went to school and got my hands on some stink bombs this guy always used in school. The stink bomb was about the size of a fifty-cent piece. No lie, those stink bombs were the worst I'd ever smelled. One whiff could stink up a whole floor at school. And I remember there were times when the dude would crack open at least ten bombs on one floor. It got so bad and overwhelming, the staff would end school early just to get everyone out. If one bomb stunk up a floor, ten bombs would make people vomit and get sick. It was the perfect way to get out of school early.

One day in May of 1990 I decided to get two stink bombs from the guy to bring home and get revenge on my father for walking Tucker around the house like a dog. Even though we were punished, we were still able to watch television. One night, Tucker and I sat on our parent's bedroom floor to watch a movie. In the middle of the movie, Levi and Kay fell asleep, and they were in a deep sleep as they were snoring away.

"Take these two stink bombs and crack them open. But before you do let me get out of your way so when the liquid spill out of the tube you can get out also," I leaned over and whispered to Tucker, as I showed him the stink bombs. Man, I was plotting the whole thing from the beginning. "Yo, I know you want to get back at Levi for treating you like a dog. These two stink bombs will stink up this whole house to the point where everybody will have to leave the house."

"For real?" He asked, taking the bombs from my hand.

After giving the stink bombs to Tucker, I quickly left out the room. It had to be like two minutes later after getting downstairs I heard Levi yell, "What's that smell!"

Tucker did not even leave out the bedroom, my brother stood up at the bottom of our parent's bed and responds, "It's a stink bomb," with a ridiculous smile upon his face. I do not know what made Tucker do it or why he did not leave the room; maybe he wanted to see the look on Levi's face when he finally smelled it. But I sat patiently at the foot of the stairs, listening to everything unfolding in our parents' bedroom.

"You know you deserve everything that's about to come to you," my mother said to Tucker as she coughed. Tucker in the meantime continued to stand at the foot of the bed laughing.

"Oh, you think this is really hilarious don't you. You come in our room and crack open a stink bomb," Levi said as he got a nice grip on his belt.

Smack was the sound of Levi's leather belt coming into contact with Tucker's skin, followed by the sound of stuff falling onto the floor. Later I found out it was from Tucker falling into the dresser and knocking almost everything off it. Next, I could hear Levi telling Tucker to take off his clothes, and as Levi gave Tucker directions, Tucker was yelling out, "Will, you set me up, man. You set me up!"

The house smelled so bad the rest of us had to sit outside. Tucker and Levi were the only ones to remain inside. From outside I could hear Tucker screaming, "My ribs, I think you broke my ribs." Once again, Levi beat Tucker so badly that night, I felt bad for giving him those stink bombs. "Will, you set me up, man. You set me up," was all he kept saying.

Levi threw Tucker down the interior steps and out of the front door. The smell continued to reek, to the point people already outside started to cover their noses. Once outside Levi told us to go back into the stinky house and open all the windows so it could air out.

With all the windows opened we went back outside, and good thing it was March as the weather was starting to warm up; otherwise, we would have frozen. Standing there looking back into the house, Levi had finally recalled what Tucker had sad, *Will you set me up*, his eyes soon took a sharp turn over to me.

Although it was a school night, almost everyone was still outside. That just how **The Hole** was. Out of the corner of my eye I saw Levi staring at me, and by his face, I knew he was starting to put two and two together. And I was thinking, *he is going to hit me out here in front of all these people.*

That's when the sleeping dragon spoke, "Will why did you bring them stinky things home to give to your brother so he could break them in our room?"

Me being me, I tried to play it cool, "I didn't know he was going to break them in your room," trying not to lower my head as he stared me down. From his stare alone, my mind was saying *stay firm*, but my body was like *run for the hills!*

"You think you're slick? You think I'm stupid, don't you?

"No. I don't think you're dumb."

"If you don't think I'm dumb, why did Tucker say, you set him up. And if you dare lie to me everybody out here will see me do something very unkindly to you," he growled through clenched teeth.

What could I say? I could not say, *Oh I brought them home because it was my way of getting back at you for the way you treat us.* Saying this would, sure enough, get me beat down. So, I tried to play it safe again, "I'm telling the truth...."

Before I could get the rest of my words out, Levi had already punched me in the stomach, causing me to buckle to the ground. I could hear Aunt B say, "Levi don't hit that boy like that again." The whole time I was folded up in a fetal position on the ground, too embarrassed to get up. I was nearly fifteen years old, and here I was still getting beatings. Moments later, Tucker came out the house holding his ribs with my other brothers following him. No matter what we did or said, it felt like getting beaten was our regular routine. With great fun, came great punishments.

It had taken months before the smell was completely out of the house, especially in my parent's bedroom. I guess, after all; I did get my payback.

A few days passed after the stink bomb incident, and when I got home from school, I found my dad had stocked up on tons of sheetrock, crowbars, hammers, nails, duct tape, sheetrock tape, and big buckets of putty. Once everyone was there, Levi said he wanted to help knock down the walls between the dining room, living room, and kitchen for an open floor plan. I believe his exact words were, "Being y'all like to be destructive, knocking down these walls should be easy," smiling.

The summer of 1990 is nearly upon us, and school would end in two months. The last few months of the school year, Walbrook High School would stay merged with Southwestern High School as the asbestos work continued. The school administration announced work would proceed through summer at Walbrook High School to remove asbestos, and students would return to Font Hill Street for the next school year. Font Hill Street was home to Southwestern High School, and Walbrook students would be joining them for another school year.

Truthfully, I did not like the idea of going to Southwestern, first of all because we always fought the dudes from there. How could I feel safe at a school where we were beefing with nearly the entire student body? We were bad, but the dudes from Southwestern simply did not care about anything. One year, someone opened fire in the school hallway. If I could not be safe in school, where could I be safe? There would be days upon days were gangs walked the halls of the school, doing what they wanted. Like Harlem Park Middle School, if you got caught slipping, you were done for.

You often smelled reefer being smoked as you walked the halls, as reefer was bought and sold on school grounds. Because of the drug trade, it was as if nearly every student had either been shot at or had shot someone. Besides the drug problem, it looked like nearly every girl at school was pregnant. In 9th grade, I wasn't all that well-known, but my boys had my back when it counted.

Southwestern and Walbrook were nearly the same. Neither school gave a fuck about the other. I tried to mind my own business, while doing my best to sex every girl I could. And truth be told, I wanted to reinvent myself. But it wasn't easy, especially since walking through the school halls always brought back memories of Harlem Park.

v Yup! You guessed it; Baltimore City Police was up there walking the halls. You would think they were looking for someone. If you know of the movie *Lean On Me*, 10 then you have an idea of what the Southwestern and Walbrook merger was like. I couldn't tell what was better—facing danger at school or dealing with boredom and beatings at home.

The weather was getting better by the day, and I could not plan anything because I was still punished. Every day once I got home from school, all my family did was knock down freaking walls The days seemed endless with carrying loads of sheetrock out of the house. We had to load trucks with all kinds of debris from the walls. The dust from knocking down the walls filled the air, covering us in layers of chalky residue. It felt like my father's demolition project went on for almost a year. I still wonder if it was a project to improve the house or his way of teaching us to appreciate what we have.

Finally, our break came when my mom asked us, "Why are Y'all always in the house?"

We all looked at her as if she had antlers growing out of her forehead. That's when Nick said, "You punished us last year remember?"

"Are you sure I punished you?"

"Yeah, we're sure you did. Matter of fact it's all our friends in the neighborhood are talking about," I answered.

"Being I forgot about it and Y'all failed to remind me. Y'all can go outside now but be back before it gets dark." By the time she had finished her sentence, we were already out the door. Speedy Gonzales had nothing on us that day.

But ain't it some shit—we've been punished so long our parents forgot they even punished us. And when they did notice we were punished, they acted like it was no big deal to let us off. To make things worse, we'd been grounded so long our friends quit knocking on the door, wondering if we could hang out.

It was like being in a new neighborhood all over again; however, I did not forget where all my friends hung out at. I went straight around to my homey Midget's house on Riggs. But there was one thing for sure concerning going around Midgets' house; you never knew what you were going to run into over their place.

One thing was clear—they were obsessed with girls, heavy and loud about it. I'd swing by sometimes (not during those eight months I was grounded, but before), and it wasn't unusual to find half-naked girls sprawled across beds or hear moaning from behind closed doors. If there weren't enough girls to go around, they'd take turns with whoever was there, no shame, no subtlety.

Most of the girls were barely out of high school—seventeen, maybe eighteen—and they seemed down for whatever. The boys didn't hold back, and the girls didn't flinch. It was wild, reckless, and way past the line, but that was the energy in that house. No rules. Just heat, noise, and a whole lot of bad decisions.

One moment burned itself into my memory like a brand. I'd swung by Midget's spot just to check in, see what he was up to. The place was quiet, but as I stepped inside, a sound cut through the stillness—low, breathy moans coming from Wendy's room. She wasn't home, but that didn't seem to matter. Boundaries blurred in that house; the only thing that mattered was the moment.

I pushed the door open and froze. The scene hit me like a punch—Test laid back, eyes half-closed, while a girl moved with purpose between his legs. Midget was behind her, locked in rhythm. It was raw, unfiltered, like something ripped straight from a late-night VHS. No shame, no hesitation. Just heat and impulse.

The door creaked open, and the girl snapped her head toward me, eyes wide like I'd caught her mid-heist. I froze—just for a beat. Was it shock? Fear? Something else? I couldn't tell. All I know is my legs took over, and I bolted— out the house, down the block, all the way home like something was chasing me. Later, after Midget wrapped up whatever he was doing, he showed up at my place and told my dad I was scared of girls. Levi took it the wrong way at first—thought Midget meant I was too shook to even talk to one or maybe to fight one. Truth was, it wasn't about the girl. It was the whole scene. The heat, the chaos, the way it cracked something open in me I wasn't ready to face.

Midget said, "Naw…. Naw, Mr. Carter. I mean Will ran from a girl that was butt naked at my house." Hearing this, Pops gave me that look—eyes sharp, locking onto me.

The first thing I thought was, *Hell Naw, I can't be about to get in trouble for this?*

That's when Levi said, "Bad as you are around this house, you mean to tell me you're afraid of a little coochie?"

"Ok, Mr. Carter don't be too hard on him. I'll make sure next time he's not afraid," continued Midget as I stood in front my father embarrassed and feeling ashamed.

After my father told me to get out of the house, all Midget did was laugh— laughing not at the thought of me being scared of having sex, but because he saw how afraid I was of my Pops. Man, when I say he laughed for hours.... he laughed for hours. Had he known the punishments and beatings Levi dealt, his laughter wouldn't have lasted long.

Now do not get me wrong, Midget did not grow up in a house with a soft parent. Yeah, Midget and his brothers were raised by their mother only, but she was not to be played with either. Her name was Ms. Peggy, and she was one tough lady. If you did anything bad around her, she would not bother to tell your parents. Instead, she would smack the hell out of you herself. She would only tell your parents about important things, like skipping school.

There was this one time—wild and unforgettable—when Ms. Peggy walked in on Nelson mid-action. The girl was sprawled out on his bed, bare as the day she was born, and Nelson was all over her like he'd lost track of the world outside that room. Ms. Peggy didn't miss a beat. She stormed in, lit into both of them with a string of curses that could peel paint off the walls.

I read the room fast. No way I was sticking around for the fallout. Mumbled something about it being late, dipped out, and didn't look back till I hit the street.

Thing is, Ms. Peggy caught us in scenes like that more than once. But she never snitched. Never called my folks. Just gave us hell and kept it moving. That's how you knew she was solid—strict when she had to be, but loyal in her own way. Yeah, she was that cool.

As I walked back home, I kept thinking how relieved I was my family had finally knocked down those damn walls. And finally, I could head straight inside and get some sleep.

When I walked in, I saw everyone sitting on the couches watching TV, so I locked the door behind me. Once in the house, I learned my brothers and I all passed to the next grade, and as a reward, my parents decided to take us to Florida for two weeks.

The summer of 1990 was a good summer to be out of Baltimore City for two weeks. I had never left the city for that long before. Eight of us went on the trip—my parents Levi and Kayden, my brothers Tucker, Quick, Nick, me, and my parents even brought my cousin Murphy and my homeboy Midget. What sticks with me about Florida back then was the crazy long ride—it took nearly eighteen hours to get there. Being a bunch of teens, it hit us the same way as getting punished.

Dad decided to take us to Florida since he had family there—an aunt and a cousin. They were Aunt Mae and our cousin Yvonne. When we arrived, we all stayed at my Aunt Mae's house for the two weeks. It was my first time meeting Aunt Mae at the age of fifteen, and instantly I knew she was an amazing person. Whenever it rained, which was nearly every day, Aunt Mae would sit around and tell us all about our family history down in Florida.

The rain in Florida was relentless, making it feel like the world was about to come to an end. The rain didn't keep us inside; nearly every day, the temperature hit 90° or higher. When the rain stopped, it got so hot we could see steam rising from the ground for thirty to forty minutes. Within five to ten minutes, the streets would dry up as if it hadn't rained at all. After the rain, snakes would come out and be everywhere. I am not sure whether or not they were poisonous, but I simply assumed they were because we were in Florida. Whatever the case maybe be, my brothers, cousin, and friend enjoyed looking at them.

So, getting back to Aunt Mae, she said Levi used to live next door, and the stairs to his place are still there, covered by long grass. "Eager to see where our father grew up, we left the house to check out the stairs. She informed us our grandfather had died in a house fire. She never said if this was why the house was gone, so I assumed it was. She told us Aunt Regina, Skylar, and Levi all had the same father. I enjoyed listening to Aunt Mae recite to us our family history, as she was the first one to tell us about it. She was also the only one who genuinely care about it.

I also had the opportunity to meet some of my other cousins while we were there. Our older cousins took us swimming and crocodile watching. But as different as it may sound, we city teenagers had fun with our big cousin Yvonne.

When I first met our cousin Yvonne, I thought she was crazy. Some of the small things she did didn't quite make sense. Yvonne would walk around talking, laughing or giggling to herself. Keep in mind, this was the first time I ever saw something so strange. But other than her weird spells, Yvonne was a good person.

When we weren't swimming or hunting crocodiles, we just kicked back and relaxed. After staying down in Florida for two weeks, we packed our bags, hopped on the road for our eighteen-hour trip, and headed back to the great city of Baltimore.

Boy oh, boy was I glad to be back in B-more! Do not misunderstand me; I enjoyed the south and spending time with unknown kinsmen and learning about my family history. But there is nothing like being home. I was now back in the comfort of my neighborhood, my block, **The Hole**.

The following day after we returned from Florida, my friend Rue got shot in the foot by K'mar using a gun Test made. This quickly became an eye opener for me as I thought to myself, *My Friends Know How to Make Guns!?* Making guns was something I thought could only be done in movies. I had friends who weren't even twenty, but they were already crafting their own weapons. I could not help but wonder where they learned these skills, but more importantly, why they needed to know them.

The police started coming around my neighborhood and down in **The Hole** after Rue got shot. I am not sure if they were looking for the weapon, the shooter, or the person who made it. And for a while, the shooting was all everyone was talking about, but through it all K'mar and Rue remained friends. It was only an accident because neither of them knew how to work that lousy gun Test put together. He made it by using an old gun frame and a pair of vice-grip pliers.

Trying to smooth things over between him and Rue, K'mar—another smooth-talking womanizer—figured the best fix was to bring Rue a girl. Ms. Sandra wasn't about to let that kind of mess go down in her house, so they posted up at Midget's spot instead. K'mar made it happen—got the girl to take care of Rue right there in the room. But just as things were heating up, in walked Ms. Peggy.

And if you knew her, you knew she didn't play. She took one look, let loose a storm of words, and kicked them all out without blinking. After that, her place was off-limits. No more late-night hangs, no more safe haven. For weeks, the crew was adrift—no spot to chill, and more importantly, no place to bring our shorties. It was like the whole scene lost its anchor.

Luckily, after a few weeks, Test was looking around the neighborhood for a bike or some parts to put one together, and he found an old tractor trailer. The trailer sat on this vacant lot at the bottom of Riggs and Payson, the doors to the trailer faced a fence and was covered with trash. As soon as Test found it, he told us he'd found a place for us to kick back and hang out.

We all followed him around to our supposed clubhouse. We had to make our way through piles of trash simply to get to the trailer. Reaching the trailer, Nelson and Test opened the doors only to find it full of all kinds of stuff. Inside the trailer were old mattresses, dressers, paper, and cement bricks that we had to clean out before using the space.

We saw the spot had potential as the hangout we needed, and just by looking at each other, we all knew what was on everyone's mind. And it was *if we wanted somewhere to chill then this was the place.*

That's when Corey said, "we gonna bring all our girls around to *Cappuccino's......*"

We all glanced his way and said, 'That's the name of our club—Cappuccinos!' It was a name a lot of the girls in the neighborhood would come to know—Cappuccinos.

All we had to do now was some major overhauling to clean it out, and it took nearly four days to do. With all the trash cleaned out of the trailer, we needed to get our hands on some beds and furniture to relax on. We fixed the problem by waiting around the neighborhood and checking yards for anyone getting rid of old furniture. If we found someone throwing out anything useful, we would grab it and carry it around to *Cappuccinos*.

On the other side of Lafayette Avenue, between Payson Street and Bentalou Street, there was an old warehouse called Acme which used to make mattresses. Sometimes they tossed out mattresses that didn't meet manufacturing standards into the dump. We often robbed those dumps of new mattresses and of course took them back to *Cappuccinos*. As the old saying goes, *your trash is another man's treasure.* Next, we figured we could not have beds without sheets, so our next move spawned an entirely new type of epidemic.

We went ALLEY SHOPPING! Yes, you read it correctly, an epidemic of Alley Shopping. It's not what it sounds like—we weren't pulling things out of the garbage. It was the exact opposite. Alley Shopping as we came to call it, was the act of walking down alleys with a trash bag. Spot something you wanted on a clothesline? You'd jump the fence, snatch the whole line down, toss it all into a trash bag, and make a run for it.

Alley Shopping became as easy as 1...2....3. From Alley shopping for sheets, we graduated to Alley Shopping for the newest and latest clothes. Grabbing all the stylish clothes our parents could not afford or were not willing to buy. It was cruel, but it was also effective for us.

As for *Cappuccino's*, the clubhouse had all kinds of blankets and sheets. Because we stole the entire clothesline, we had a stash of bra's, panties, t-shirts, pants, tennis, coats, and jackets. It did not matter what it was. At the time if we wanted it, it was ours. There were a few times when I would be around other peers and hear them talking about how their clothesline had been cut down. During situations like this, I would simply remain quiet, and think to myself, *how unfortunate it is for you,* as they went on talking.

There was this one time I went alley shopping, and I hit this yard with all the latest clothes I wanted. There were Jordache Pants, Nike T-shirts, a clothing line called Used by Perry Ellis and some Mickey Mouse blankets. I had to take the whole line! I jumped over the fence and stole everything. My parents started thinking I was dealing drugs since I stayed looking sharp, but I told them my friends were hooking me up with their old clothes.

With a fresh set of clothes and shoes about every week or so, I noticed all the girls at school and in the neighborhood started loving me, and I was in return loving it. So, to keep it going, I needed to keep on alley shopping, but this time, I had to hit lines outside of the neighborhood as people in the neighborhood started hearing of lines being cut down. But this was only part of the truth. I also started going out of the neighborhood because I did not want to cut somebody's clothesline down I knew, but for all the lines I had cut it, was bound to happen eventually.

This moment came while I was hanging out on the corner, and the clothes-line I hit last week—full of Eli gear—turned out to belong to a girl who was standing right there. She said, "Will are they're my pants you have on?" These pants were $90 in the store but for what reason? The denim jeans came with rips and patches, but they were designer.

I had no choice but to respond, "NO Bitch! What the fuck I look like having your pants on for?" That was all I could say. No way I was letting people find out I was one of the main ones out here stealing clothes. By this time, I was known for being fresh, and I could not let this ruin my reputation.

However, she was not trying to allow the situation of dying down and continued by saying, "You stole them off my line last week. And I can tell their mine by the ink stain on the back pocket."

Now I felt like a true ass, as I turned to look at the back pocket and damn if she was not correct. Directly on the right back, pocket was an ink stain. Everybody on the corner started laughing as my face twisted to show my embarrassed expression as I looked at the stain. With my reputation now flying out of the window with their laughs, I turned and popped the girl right in the eye for disrespecting me.

While she stood there in pain, holding the eye I had punched, her girlfriends came at me, trying to jump me. No doubt I got the hell out of there and ran home, took off the pants and took them to the cleaners. The next time someone would see me in them, they would not be pants but a pair of shorts.

She had the nerve! Trying to disrespect me in front of people. That was a definite no-go. But with me no longer alley shopping in my neighborhood, situations such as this was no longer an issue.

And to help with my lack of high-end clothes, there was this truck which started selling cheaper gear around the way. The truck would come around to the Super Pride Market lot on Payson Street, only a block away from Cappuccinos. Tyrone, who owned the truck, had all the newest styles.

We used to go down to Tyrone's truck and act like we were going to buy something. We would spot a few things we liked on his tables, and when he was not paying attention to us, we would snatch it off the table and run. Tyrone would chase us for a bit, but he always stopped once he realized the rest of his stuff was still out on the tables.

After robbing Tyrone of the goods, we would all meet back up at Cappuccino's and hide out there. Tyrone flagged down the police and pointed in the direction we had taken off. From inside the trailer of Cappuccino's we could hear police chatter over their walkie-talkies as they walked around the neighborhood looking for us. The cops walking past Cappuccino's felt like they were out there forever, but things finally chilled once they couldn't find us.

To this day, I still wonder what our charges would've been if we had gotten caught—grand theft, breaking and entering the trailer, and stealing all the goods stashed inside? After everything we did in the trailer, Cappuccino's started getting talked about all over the hood, especially in **The Hole**. The only thing missing from Cappuccinos was a neon sign.

CHAPTER FIVE: THE CONSEQUENCE

Now my mind comes to the day of October 2, 1991, the day of my parents' anniversary and the day before my 16th birthday. On this particular day, I decided to cut out of school because some older dude was selling us a *Street Sweeper*, which is another name for a 12-gauge pistol grip shotgun.

For some odd reason we thought we needed a gun, so we got one. After we hooked school and went to purchase the gun, we headed to Midget's house to check out and inspect our newly purchased item.

Soon as we stepped inside, we headed straight for the basement. Ms. Peggy never came down there—why, I couldn't tell you. Maybe it was the damp, maybe the dust, maybe she just knew better. Either way, it was our safe zone. K'mar, Midget, and I posted up, huddled around the shotgun like it was some sacred relic. First one in our stash. We'd already stacked ten handguns, but this felt different—heavier, louder, more serious. We were buzzing, trying to crack open the rear chamber, fingers slick with sweat and frustration. But no matter how we twisted or pried, the damn thing wouldn't budge. It sat there, stubborn and silent, like it knew we weren't ready for what came next.

I turned to K'mar and said, "Let me hold it." After I'd done everything I could—or thought I could—to get the damn gun to work, I handed it back to K'mar in frustration.

K'mar seemed to know a little more about guns as he was the one who had them most often. That's when Nelson came down the basement and wanted to see the gun. Bored and frustrated with the shit, I turned around to watch the Price Is Right.

That's when I heard Nelson say, "Y'all dumb as shit! How Y'all can't open the chamber...."

BOOOOOM!

Then it happened—the worst thing imaginable. The gun went off. I had my back to them when it hit, tearing into my right shoulder blade. The blast was so close, the pellets punched straight through me and blew out my chest. Point-blank. I didn't even register the shot at first. No sound, no sting—just a blank space where my body used to be. Then, seconds later, the pain came crashing in. And it wasn't just pain—it was pure, unfiltered agony. Like my nerves had been set on fire from the inside out. I've taken some brutal beatings from Levi in my time, and I won't lie—he knew how to hurt a man. But this? This made every one of those feel like a slap on the wrist.

I drifted through the basement in a daze, everything slowed and surreal, like I'd slipped into someone else's nightmare. The television flickered in front of me, and I just stared—blood from my chest tracing a slow, dark line down the screen. A few seconds passed. I tried to stand, tried to move, whispering to myself, This isn't real. This can't be happening. But then the coughing started—violent, unstoppable. My lungs seized as blood surged upward, thick and choking. It spilled from my mouth in heavy black clots, each one tasting like rust and regret. That metallic tang still lingers in my memory. Like the moment branded itself into my bones.

K'mar and Nelson were already bolting up the basement steps by the time I turned to face them. Everything had unraveled in seconds, but for that first minute, time felt warped—like the world had dropped into slow motion. I staggered, reaching for the cold concrete wall to steady myself. It was slick beneath my palm, unforgiving. My shoulder dragged along it as I leaned in, smearing a dark trail of blood across the gray surface. Each breath felt heavier, each second louder, like the basement itself was holding its breath with me.

Though my shirt clung to me, heavy and warm with blood, a strange chill crept over my skin—like the basement itself had turned against me. I slid along the wall, each step jagged and uneven, my legs trembling beneath me. My knees buckled, strength draining like water through a cracked pipe. It felt like someone had strapped fifty-pound weights to my feet. Every movement was a battle. I was slipping—fast. My vision flickered, my thoughts stuttered, reality blinking in and out like a dying lightbulb.

It was then I heard Midget saying, "Please Will don't die on me." His words sounded muffled as if he was speaking through an inch of glass.

I tried my best and hardest to make it to the top of the basement stairs when things finally went black. When I finally came back to consciousness, I was in the back of an ambulance. While unconscious, I started having flashbacks to different periods of my life, the good and bad. There were flashbacks where my brothers and I were wrestling. There were times when I was getting chased by gang members. Then it there came times when I was with my parents having an awesome time.

Then there came a deep voice, not in my natural ear but somehow speaking to my subconscious repeating, "I need you."

Maybe it was the Lord's voice? It was followed by the brightest light I have ever seen. It was like looking into a thousand suns. The light is something beyond what words can capture. The voice and light started to fade in and out until I heard a set of different voices, saying, "We're losing him, we're losing him. SHOCK!"

I felt myself raise up out of my body and was able to see the paramedics were working on me. They had the defibrillator pressing against my chest, as they shouted, "Clear!"

As I stood beside the paramedics, one of them, looking down at my lifeless body, said, "He has FLATLINED!"

"Pronounce the time," said a blonde EMS.

"1:41 pm," responded the other EMS.

The out-of-body sensation was terrifying—like I'd slipped out of time, hovering somewhere between here and whatever comes next. Across the ambulance, through the haze of blood and flashing lights, I saw him: a blurred figure of a man, arms stretched wide, standing still as stone. Behind it all, the flatline screamed from the monitor, sharp and steady. The EMTs were talking, voices low and urgent, but their words felt distant—like echoes from another world I was no longer part of.

But the deep calm voice spoke to me and said, "I'm not through with you... PLEASE!"

Believe me when I say this is not fabricated. I had to be the only one who could see this man because the EMS folks did not pay attention to this Guy! I was so-so scared. I was only fifteen years old, and I was about to die the day before my birthday. As the ambulance pulled off from the curb and turned on the emergency lights to speed its way to the hospital, I continued to see the blurred vision of the man. I know this shit sounds crazy to you because it sounds crazy to me, but this is true. Although I couldn't see his face, I knew he was looking directly at me, and I felt it deep in my soul. The man looked at me and said, "I'll return when you are ready! Your job here is not complete."

I attempted to ask the man a question by repeating, "WHY ME? WHY ME? By this time, I was back to consciousness and laying on the bed of the ambulance, repeating those same words, "WHY ME?"

At this point, one of the EMS yells, "We have a pulse, we have a pulse. His heart is pumping!"

Suddenly my eyes jolted open, and I saw the paramedics going to work on my young body. For the remainder of my trip to the hospital, I faded in and out, but I was ALIVE!

The EMS people continually slapped me in the face, asking me one question after another, saying, "Do you know your name? Do you know today's date? Do you know the year?" I have no doubts those slaps kept me from fading completely out. But unfortunately, the last thing I heard from one of them was, "Hello! Do you know what happened to you?"

My mind immediately slipped back into limbo, showing me flashbacks of past events. It started with images of my parents' wedding. I saw Reverend Odenton running up the aisle as he preached, followed by images of Felesha. Next came my mother's beautiful face—but no images of my father. Where is he? Why no flashes of him?

I was shot in the back by my so-called friends who all ran out on me. I was only fifteen, and on the following day of October 3, 1991, I was turning sixteen, and my father Levi was going to be thirty-four. My thoughts turned to resentment as I started thinking in this state of limbo, how my friends killed me the day before my sixteenth birthday. What a birthday gift to my father and myself, before I knew it, I had faded completely. A world of blackness.... A

68

world of nothing.... FLATLINE.

The story now goes Levi went straight crazy upon hearing the news. He did not learn the news of me being shot until after he came home from work. Levi loaded both his guns and went out searching for Nelson and K'mar, since everyone claimed they were the ones who shot me and left me for dead.

What an anniversary day my parents had. Work all day, expect to come home and celebrate a special day; instead, you hear your oldest son was shot by his friends and he possibly may not survive the night. No one knew my parents' phone numbers in case there was ever an emergency, but finally, someone remembered my Aunt B. lived next door to us.

I was shot around 1:30 pm during a time I should have been in school. When word surfaced K'mar and Nelson had killed me in the basement of Midget's house, it became an all-out manhunt. The police had already locked Midget up, although he was the only one who stayed back and attempted to help me live. Everyone else had given up when I was laying on my back unconscious with blood spewing from my mouth and pouring out of my back like a river. By staying back, Midget was the only one who still believed I deserved to keep living.

They say K'mar ran all the way down Edmondson Avenue and Pulaski Street, which was nearly a good mile away from where I nearly died. He told the older guys, "I think my homeboy Nelson killed Will."

I guess he was frantic in his statements as everyone he talked to tried to calm the little fella down. "K'mar....K'mar....K'mar, calm down! Where's Will now," they asked him.

"He's in the basement dead from the *Street Sweeper* we got from Shank!" K'mar continued to yell.

"Well, if Will got shot by the *Street Sweeper* Shank sold you guys, your friend Will is dead. No doubt bout that," said his friends.

A *Street Sweeper* is any high-powered gun with a large ammo capacity (lit. Uzi, Mac-10, Ak-47, etc.), so when you begin to shoot, it sweeps the street.

If you were to stand on one end of the block and shoot the high-powered weapon, the rounds/pellets would hit everything without having to reload soon after. In my case it happened to be a shotgun, from which the pellets in the cartridge would spread open after being fired, allowing it to hit more targets if necessary. Unfortunately for me, the pellets did not have the chance to spread, being I was at close range. With the pellets not spreading, it was like being shot or hit with a baseball going 300 miles per hour, ripping my shoulder blade from my back upon contact.

Reaching the hospital, I was immediately taken into the operating room and laying there on the table; I thought about the prospects of my brothers living on without me. The mere thought was enough to send me back into shock. I guess your mind is your health after all.

"He's flat lining.... He's flat lining," is all I could hear as I started to fade away. They immediately rushed me back into the operating room. It was a weird and unexplainable thing to hear people speaking around me but being unable to feel, respond or move. I could hear the doctors yell, "Clear" as they hit me with the defibrillator, but the funny thing was in the fact I could not feel the shock. I guess the Lord spared me from the pain as well.

The sequence of hearing them yelling, "Clear" and hitting me over and over with the defibrillator seemed to last forever as they tried to jump start my heart. It's strange how your heart can stop beating for over a minute, but your mind continues to press on, thinking of all the *what ifs* in life.' Maybe this is what they call the soul. I lay there motionless, but my mind was running a marathon, thinking over those *what ifs*. Mainly, *what if I only stayed in school, would this ever happen to me? Am I dead or alive?*

It was a constant battle of the mind and body as I faded in & out, and over the next seven months, I continued to go through multiple procedures and operations.

Following my shooting, and in fear of getting caught K'mar made his way down E.A (Edmonson Avenue) to so-called hide out from the police, I later learned it did not take the police too long before they found K'mar. I think they said they had him within five days after the shooting. After heavy interrogation, they let K'mar go realizing he was not the actual one who pulled the trigger.

Soon after K'mar's release, Nelson turned himself into the police because his conscience had got to him. They kept Nelson in custody and at any given moment they were waiting to charge him with murder once word came back from the hospital I had died. Good thing that word never came, or I would not be sitting here explaining this story, My Story, to you. The doctors sent the word out announcing they had brought me back to life and stabilized me.

As I sit before you now, I want to let you know I was given a second chance at life, one which eventually allowed me to bring you into this world, son. I still had a long way to go! But it was not easy; I still had to go on and continue to fight for my life. I turned sixteen years old as I lay on the operation room bed the following day. What a hell of a present for myself! So many operations and procedures to go through.

While I was in the hospital fighting for my life, Nelson was in prison fighting for his freedom. I am not saying the struggles were the same; damn if those be my words. I'm just saying it must have been tough for him to be alone in prison, knowing his sentence could last a lifetime if I didn't survive. Fighting against himself mentally, knowing he killed me by a mere incident. He would remain in jail for as long as I was in the hospital.

On the outside, I later heard my father Levi went crazy out there. Some say he told Ms. Peggy he planned to shoot up their house if I died, and Midget would definitely die, even though he was the only one who tried to save me. Levi did not care, and I guess he did care about us. My mother was torn to pieces. How could she deal with the fact her oldest boy was shot dead the day of their anniversary and a day before his sixteenth birthday? My mother Kayden was still young herself, only being thirty-one years old. How could I bring her and thirty-four old Levi this much pain? My little brothers did an amazing job at being strong for our parents and me, showing their support as best they knew how.

CHAPTER SIX: THE THOUGHTS

It was May 1992 when I finally fully opened my eyes to see my mother and father's faces staring down at me, their eyes filled with joy and praise. I knew they loved me and missed me as I must have looked like a creature from a science fiction movie lying on a suspended bed with all sorts of attachments and tubes running from me.

At first, I was unable to speak because of the large plastic tube running down my throat, used to feed me. I had a catheter running down through my penis to assist with my urination. Holes in the floor blew in medicated air, ensuring the wounds on my back and chest stayed free from infection. It was strange as I could not move any part of my body except for my eyes.

For the first time in my life, I looked over and saw my father crying. I figured something really bad must have happened as my father is the toughest person or should I say, man, I knew of. He was like a rock, and like a rock, it took a lot to break him. I thought to myself, *Levi doesn't cry! He makes people cry!*

Being I could not talk, my mother placed a pad under my hand and placed a pencil between my fingers. The next thing I did was one of the most difficult things I have ever done, and I could easily compare it to attempting to climb Mount Everest. I tried my best to write while lying flat on my back and after several attempts all I accomplished were scribbled lines stating nothing. And even through this tough struggle, I did not give up. I continued to press on because I had to know what was bothering my father.

Finally, after retraining the muscles in my hand, I was able to write, "Why is Levi crying and why am I in the hospital?"

That's when I watched my mother break down crying like she had never done before and asked me, "You don't remember do you?"

I responded by writing down on the pad, "no."

That's when out of nowhere a doctor entered the room and accidentally dropped their clipboard to the floor.

BOOOOM!

The sound triggered a flashback to seven months earlier, making me fully realize this wasn't a dream—I had been shot by my friend and left on the floor to die.

"Will, it may not seem like it, but you have been asleep since October last year, seven months ago. And now it's May 1992," my mother explained.

I remember thinking, *Wow!* I survived a coma! While I was in the coma, I had multiple skin grafts; I had muscle taken out of my right leg and placed into my back. I had thirty staples in my chest to help keep the wound closed after the shotgun blast opened it up. A wad of cotton balls was placed on my back to soak in a solution helping fight off infections. In addition to everything else I endured during the coma, I received multiple blood transfusions. But most importantly I had the Lord on my side.

Every day following my awakening from a seven-month coma, I simply lay in bed and absorbed everything which had happened in my young life. And son, I tell you, when there's nothing else to think about or do, you have no choice but to reflect on your life and the decisions you have made—it forces you to reconsider your actions. Months ago, I was running around the streets like any other teenager, chasing after girls and hanging out with my friends just like you do today. But it was taken away from me in an instant—the very instant the shotgun fired.

A week or two later I was in the I.C.U (Intensive Care Unit) and the doctor could no longer hold it in anymore as he came to me, "Mr. Carter," he said compassionately. From the look on his face, I knew what he was about to say next could not be good. "Mr. Carter," he continued, "from the way things look and the intensity of your trauma, we and I mean as in my team of doctors and me have concluded there is a strong possibility you will be quadriplegic."

What is that, I thought to myself.

"Pellets from the shotgun hit your spine, damaging nerves and muscle function. I am sorry to say you will be paralyzed from the neck down."

I immediately started praying to my Lord; *NO......this can't be.* But my chance to pray did not last long as the doctor quickly brought me back to reality. Reality was turning out to be Hell on Earth.

"Mr. Carter most likely over time there is a strong possibility you will become a paraplegic," he continued. "You'll be able to move everything above the waist, but nothing below."

In other words, he was saying I would not be able to walk again. I was torn on the inside, physically and mentally. I could see on my parents' faces how terrible a mistake I had made by cutting out of school on 10/02/91. I would be paralyzed at the age of fifteen, and yet I had so much to live for. I had so much unfinished work ahead of me.

June of 1992 had arrived, and I was shot eight months ago! The only difference now was I was able to sit up with no help, but moving my legs was out of the question. At the end of the month, I had started therapy. They were hoping this would efficiently teach me how to use my upper strength to replace my non-functioning lower body.

My physical therapy doctor name was Debbie. I will never forget her. She was a white petite blonde lady. Debbie, or should I say, Mrs. Debbie, was so cute in the face, but she had no *ass-ah-tall.* You get it, no ass at all! I was tripping because I could not do anything for this lady but get well. However, by the end of July, Dr. Debbie released me to *Montebello Rehabilitation Outpatient Center.*

Upon my arrival at the center, two police came to my room with all their folders and documentation in hand and stood on the left-hand side of the foot of my bed. The one standing to my left greeted me first, "Hello Mr. Carter. My name is Sgt. Anders, and this is Sgt. Johnson," pointing to the other officer. "We're glad to see and hear you are feeling better."

"Thank you," I responded.

"I and Sgt. Johnson are not going to waste your time, so we are going to get straight to the point," he said with a hint of authority, looking deep into my eyes. "We currently are holding the individual by the name of Nelson Garner in custody, and we've been holding him since your accident. We were waiting until we completely found out the status of your condition. Because we did not know how to charge him with the act of shooting you and if that charge was going to turn into a case of murder."

To this day, I can picture the look on my pops' face when I told him to release Nelson. It was a look of admiration for looking out for my friend, mixed with the thought he should still end Nelson's life.

I was slowly able to say the words, "I don't want to press charges." As hard as it was to say those words, deep down I knew it was truly a mistake, even though he nearly killed me. *I would have died from a simple mistake.* The thought of it hit home; I pictured myself being in a casket all laid up with the best suit my parents could afford for me. A tear dropped from my eye. *Why couldn't they have been more careful with the gun? What if I would have died?* I did not understand the statement at the time, but how could they have been more careful? They were only teenagers. We were only teenagers.

The police had Nelson now for nine months, and now it was all riding on me if he were to be a free teenager or not. If I say otherwise my friend would not see the outside until he was an adult. Did I want to do this? With all the strength within me, I stuck to my initial statement. I did not want to press charges. The officers took my statement, then left the room, but not before explaining Nelson would remain locked up because of his possession of a gun.

I wanted to give up on life so many times during this period. I was emotional, torn apart in body, mind, and spirit—ripped wide open the way the shotgun had torn through my flesh and bone, leaving nothing untouched in its wake

Why me Lord? Why have I gone through so much at one time at such a young age?

With months of being away from my family while in Montebello Rehabilitation Outpatient Center, I started having psychotic thoughts as I recovered. I no longer had the desire to live, especially since my ability to walk was gone. What teenager does not want to have a life of placing one foot before the other to get around? I began blaming the world. I wanted to bring the pain I was suffering to others. My mind started to lose a grip on reality, my mood and behavior started to change drastically, as I often suffered from symptoms of delusions and hallucinations. I cried every day and night to myself and the Lord. It was a very dark time in my life and the pain I endured, no tear could ever explain the sorrow I felt and thought.

I got shot when I was fifteen years old and woke up when I was sixteen, nearly a year later. The weight of this alone caused me to start hating God. I could not help but think he allowed this to happen to me, it was His fault. I was so angry at God, when I verbally told Him, "If I ever walk again, I am going to walk into any of your churches and shoot the MUTHA FUCKA up!"

I had thoughts of walking into a funeral, right up to the front where the family of the deceased would be with a big ass automatic in one hand and a forty-four magnum in the other hand and looking them up and down. Before I released every shot loaded in my guns, I would look to the sky and say, "God make room because I have an entire family coming your way." Then BOOM! BOOM! POP! POP! Were all those individuals would hear last.

Yeah, I was full of the Devil and devilish thoughts, but who could blame me? I was sixteen and paralyzed because I was shot by a freaking 20-gauge shotgun in the back. I had so much pain inside me after being shot in which no medication could take away. Death was the only thing I ever thought about, and believing it would be my only release. There was no life for anyone if I had anything to do with it. *Why did I have so much pain in me? Only God and that gunshot knew.* I had started looking at people as targets. They were moving targets the Lord had put in front of me to kill.

I no longer wanted the pain I was feeling and to stop it here, I needed somebody else to feel it. And the only thing which kept me from fulfilling my agreement of hurting others was the simple fact I could not walk. The Lord knew the day I learned to walk would be the day many innocent people lost their lives.

The doctors told my parents that everything I experienced had caused me to become psychotic. I remember thinking, *these whores ain't see psychotic. Hell, wait till I come back in this bitch and kill half the staff.* I was thinking this because I wanted them to feel my pain! The dream and nightmares I had every night would have made the average person go crazy as well.

So, ask yourself, son, what does crazy look like in the mind of a lunatic? I don't know if the physical therapy was working or not. They would have me lay on my back, and then, they would lift one of my legs at a time. Repeating this procedure, a total of ten times for each leg. I honestly did not give the therapy my all as my mind was focused on thoughts of killing a mutha fucka! Yeah, I was mentally screwed up!

If the shotgun blast had disabled my ability to walk, I was wondering why they were still sending me to Montebello for therapeutic treatment. I came close to having the means to end my life, but the chance slipped further away each time they shuffled me through different rooms in the building, day after day. After spending six months in Montebello, they finally discharged me into the outpatient unit, which did nothing for me but get me a larger hospital bill. At the end of December 1992, I was discharged to my home where this all started, **The Hole!**

Upon going home, my parents sent me to live with my Grandmother Laura on Winchester Street instead of home. I only stayed with her a short time because I was too heavy for her lift. I cried to myself often, as I could not do shit for myself. The only reason I had to stay with my grandma and not at home was because my parents had to work Monday through Friday every week and they could not afford to take off from work.

I needed help around the clock 24/7, and there was nothing my grandmother could do for me, except feed me. I needed someone not only to feed me, but also to change my diaper, change my sheets, clean my poop, and put me in the tub to bathe me. After a short time with Grandma Laura, my parents moved me to live with my father's mother, Grandma Inas. I could not help but love Grandma Laura for at least trying to help me. I have to admit I missed her cooking after I left. Even though I was staying with Grandma Ina, I wished I could have spent more time with Grandma Laura.

While living with Grandma Laura, I had the opportunity to bond with my cousin Raw, who came by nearly every day to check on me. Ever since we moved out of Grandma Laura's house and onto Appleton Street in 1988, I did not spend as much time with him. Raw had also become my personal barber and did not allow my hair to grow longer than one week.

Living on Winchester Street with my grandma came with other perks, including having some attractive neighbors. Ms. Sally lived on my grandma's left and to her right was Ms. Lo-Lo and Mr. Hurp.

Ms. Sally had four kids, two boys Aaron and Larry, and two girls, Tiffany and Dena. Tiffany was beyond sexy to me, like her mother. I never told Tiffany I had a crush on her because Aaron would have no doubt tried to beat me up. Aaron always looked at my little brothers and me as if we were his brothers. However, most of the time Aaron stayed locked up from selling drugs and hanging with them glue sniffers.

While Aaron was in and out of jail, I never built up the heart to tell Tiffany how I felt about her. Tiffany had a presence that turned heads—tall, graceful, with warm brown eyes and long flowing hair. There was something magnetic about her, the kind of beauty that made people pause. You had to see her in person to really understand. Over time, she started calling me her little brother. And I won't lie—I loved Tiffany. Deep down, that nickname meant something to me. It made me feel seen, protected. But what I cherished most was when she'd show up at my grandma's house just to check on me. No fanfare, no reason—just making sure I was okay. That kind of care stuck with me.

Larry and Dena were younger than I was and were around the age of my younger brother Quick. Tucker was older than them both. I would have still played with Larry and Dena growing up, but the opportunity never presented itself.

Ms. Lo-Lo lived next door on the right side of my grandma's house. Her daughter Crystal was about my age, and she had two younger sisters—Myra and the baby of the bunch, Victoria. Crystal always had a thing for me. Can't blame her—I was easy on the eyes back then, and I knew it.

When Grandma Laura sat in the kitchen, she would normally be in there for a while, and while she would be in there getting dinner together, Crystal would come over. Crystal would enter through the back door, knowing Grandma was always in the kitchen nearby, while I couldn't get up to answer the front door. After checking on my grandma and making sure she had everything she needed, Crystal would come into the room and sit with me. She often told me how strong I was to come this far after getting shot. And would often make fun of me and say things like, "that's why your thing doesn't work."

Since I struggled with talking after being shot, all I could do was smile at Crystal's wild antics. She'd check my diaper and play around with my little man constantly—almost like it became her little hobby for a while, the way she kept doing it. I think she was trying to see if she could be the first to get me aroused again. Man, I loved when Crystal came to visit.

During one of her visits, Crystal leaned in close and joked that she always messed with me because, one day, she planned to take things further. For the first time in what felt like forever, I cracked a real smile—one of those rare ones that came from deep inside. She caught it and smiled back, like we both knew something had shifted. Even though it was hard to get the words out, I couldn't help myself. I looked at her and said, "Bet you won't suck it."

I guess it was something she always wanted to do because she got excited. Taking my little man in her hands, she gave me the business while looking up into my eyes. I didn't have to worry about my grandma walking in on us since her arthritis made her legs slow, and we could hear her coming from a mile away. A walker and squeaky floors are not a good combination if you want to sneak up on someone.

Crystal then took off her shirt and bra, showing off her pretty ass titties. She stopped sucking on me and said, "that's enough for now." She then sat back on the couch, took off her pants and panties, propped both legs wide open on the couch, and without hesitation she started pleasuring herself. She did this until she made herself orgasm. This blew my mind! And as if it was a normal thing, she got back up and put on her clothes, then whispered in my ear, "I don't want to be playing with myself forever. I need you to get better so get that dick of yours to work and then we can finally do something fo'real," she finished with a smile.

"Girl you crazy," I responded.

And before she left for the day, she would always kiss me on the cheek and suck me one more time, and say to my privates, "I'll see you very soon." I would then hear her talking to my grandma a bit longer, telling her she changed me and powdered me down. Of course, she would never tell her how she powdered me down or of herself masturbation. This went on with Crystal and me for the entire three weeks I was there at Grandma Laura's house. Sometimes I wondered if my grandma knew about the things Crystal was doing to me. And if she did know, she never showed any signs.

At the end of the third week, I was waiting and wishing for Crystal to hurry up and come, I needed my daily change. Not only did Crystal not show up, but my parents came over and told me they were taking me over to stay with Grandma Inas' now. My mother explained to me while I was over Grandma Inas' house, Dennis, my father's old friend would be taking care of me while they were at work, and I would be getting home tutoring by the Baltimore Public School System.

Yo! I was so mad. First, they were taking me away from Crystal and from all the extra things she would do to me. I did not even get the chance to say thanks for everything or tell her goodbye.

On Sunday, December 27, 1992, I went to live with my other grandmother over in East Baltimore. God damn I was going to miss living with Grandma Laura. I never knew if she knew I was going to be leaving, and if she did, like always she never showed it.

On Monday, January 4, 1993, I began my tutorial schooling. I'm not sure whether my silence was caused by a physical or mental block; all I know is I started talking more—at least more than I had in the past year or so.

My tutor was an old black lady by the name of Mrs. Lopaz. I thought only Mexicans had these names. The truth is she was married to a Mexican dude. She told me after I asked her about her last name. Mrs. Lopaz came to my Grandma Inez's house from 12 pm to 4 pm and taught me math and reading on Mondays, science and social studies on Tuesdays, math again on Wednesdays, and Thursdays we went over languages. Fridays were usually reserved for make-up or review.

Every morning around 9:00 am, when I needed to bathe, Dennis would carry me up the stairs to the tub. He was a strong little man, and he made it look easy to carry me up and down the steps as he wore his weightlifter's belt. I did not like Dennis or my father washing me up because they were men, and I surely did not want any of my cousins to bathe me. Truth be told I did not want my grandmother or mother washing me up being I had now hit puberty. The only real candidate for the job was Crystal, but she was all the way over in West Baltimore, and I was stuck in East Baltimore. I had to suck in the fact I had no other choice but to have Dennis do the job.

One positive aspect was my ability to control certain motor functions and move my upper body to some degree, enabling me to wash certain parts of my body on my own. Dennis would wash the other areas and around my wounds. Dennis would sit me in the tub after he had undressed me....Ewww! No Homo! I do thank God for Dennis and the time he spent with me. Without him I would have been one filthy ass nigga, pardon my French.

Being over in East Baltimore I started to miss my brothers. They continued to live in West Baltimore down in **The Hole**, and I had no way of seeing them except when Kayden or Levi brought them over to visit. How sad! I had only my bad ass cousin Lil Bobby a.k.a Ray, to keep me company, and he was only four or five years old.

While over there, I found it weird how everyone would teach him how to curse. Like if you say, "Hey come here." Someone else in the room with you might say to him, "Lil Ray say fuck you." Or if you say, "Lil Ray bring me such uh such," he would automatically reply, "Hell Naw!" We would all laugh at this, which only encouraged him to curse more.

As stupid as it may sound, we continued to teach him how to curse. I obviously could not teach him these bad words when the adults were around, but I did my fair share of teaching.

Anyway, after I had finished up in the tub, Dennis would come and help me put my clothes on. He often sprayed me with some of his expensive cologne and would buy me the latest clothes to put on. I guess he did it to help bring up my spirit, and it did a little, but I still thought often of suicide deep down inside. My Grandma Inas gave me my pain medication of 30mg of Percocet every few hours, which made me feel great. However, after the feeling wore off, I was still stuck with the reality of not being able to walk.

I remember constantly telling the Lord if I ever walked again, I was going to kill somebody. This old pain would not subside. I wanted to let somebody else feel my pain; everyone around me knew I was paralyzed, but none of them knew how it felt to be paralyzed. I was fifteen years old the day I got shot, a day before my birthday, the infamous date of October 2, 1991, the day of my parents' three-year anniversary. The sad thing was I did not know I was shot until eight months later, but being told I was shot was not the hardest news to receive. Being told I would never walk again tore me down into **The Hole**.

Now I think about it, I did not walk for over a year and a half. I was able to move the upper torso, and some may have considered this a blessing to be able to do so. But what the hell? I still couldn't walk; how in the hell was this a blessing? When family and friends brought me over food, clothing and gifts, I still thought of murder. When I received kisses and cards encouraging me to keep up the fight, I still thought of only death.

Not many people know and understand what it is like to lay there in bed crying while talking to the Lord. I used to pray and curse the Lord out in the same breath, and truthfully, it all depended on how I felt at the moment. I figured he still heard me if he was always listening, right? My actual prayers went a little like this:

Lord why me? Why the fuck ME! Why the fuck am, I paralyzed at a young age? Why was I the chosen one out of that group to be reprimanded? Why must I feel this damn pain all the time? Lord if I ever walk again, I will bring down havoc, destruction, devastation, ruinous damage to someone and their family! They will come to feel the pain the same way that I do…. they will feel it!

Yes, there was a time I thought about Nelson! There were also times I thought about K'mar. Crazy thoughts used to come into my mind about the best way to bring them to death. Being Midget stayed back to help me up out of the basement, I figured I would spare his life.

At this point in my life, I knew and understood I was a confused teen, carrying something inside me that one day everyone would see.

One good thing about staying at my grandma's house in East Baltimore was having the chance to see my father's side of the family much more. My cousin Candy, Lisa, Stan, Hailey, Orenda, Murphy, and Serena all came around pretty often. But even with them around to bring a smile to my face, DEATH continued to stay on my side, or should I say, on my mind.

It was not long after I was released from home tutorial classes and was back on the Westside with my brothers. When I moved back in with my brothers, my parents had decided I could sleep in the basement as the basement gave me more privacy and space to maneuver me around. My brothers Quick and Nick shared the middle room while Tucker had the back room. I guess it was done to give us all some degree of privacy.

Although the basement was mine, I didn't sleep there immediately because it was cool and damp, and my back was still open. Levi did not want to chance it getting infected, so he set up the living room with a television and a large round sofa with four pillows. The sofa was comfortable, but it was no bed. Soon after, Dennis gave me his old waterbed after he had purchased a new one.

Since I was back on the west side, I had so many friends from Walbrook High School come through to see me. They were always good to see, as it was nice to look upon familiar faces. **The Hole** was where I needed to be! I got to see all my old friends I had not seen in over a year. With old friends in mind, I started wondering, *did anybody find my 9mm down in the basement ceiling?* Man, if it was still down there, there were going to be some murders when I became right. For the moment, fate had me confined to a damned bed or wheelchair.

Yeah, that was my LIFE....

In those confined spaces, I would curse the Lord out as I saw and heard the kids run up and down the streets. But there were also times I thanked him for my health. This new health would give me the opportunity to repay certain friends who had imposed this confined life on me.

February 3, 1993, was my Cousin Raw's eighteenth birthday. And it was also the day when my mom told me I could now stay in the basement. I looked at my mother with a puzzled face, trying to figure out what the rush was. But it was not to long after I learned Grandma Laura would be living with us.

My father carried me down into the basement so I could check it out and see how I wanted to have things set up. My father Levi knew a lot about houses, so it was nothing to him to insulate the windows in the basement.

As we descended into the basement, I glanced over to the spot where my gun was stashed in the ceiling. I wondered why Grandma Laura was coming to live with us; she had her house on Winchester Street. Getting her to come live with us would not have been easy as she lived on Winchester Street for thirty plus years. I figured it was a fishy thing she would give up the privacy of her home to stay in our living room. It had me thinking, *did she give up everything to accommodate my needs? Was she leaving her house because she was getting up in age? What, she could not afford to stay by herself anymore?*

I had all kinds of thoughts running through my mind at this point. Then I thought, *what if someone tried to break in my grandmother's house and almost harmed her or maybe they did harm her?* I was getting stressed over not knowing the situation.

My thoughts were shattered when Levi told me the only reason, I had to come out of the living room so early was because Grandma Laura needed to live with us. But I could see in my father's eyes there was something more than her simply moving in.

Looking into his eyes, I had to ask, "Why is Grandma moving out of her house and with us?" The pain reflected in his eyes when I asked that question brought back memories of my time in the I.C.U. Levi's next few words altered my life forever.

"Will, there is no other way to put this. Will, your Grandmother Laura has lung cancer, and the doctor gave her only three months to live."

WHAT THE FUCK!!! OH, MY GOD!!!

If my mind was already fucked up, this sure was not going to help it. I could not go on living with the thought of my grandmother not being around. I was helpless at doing anything for myself, and now my grandma was sick, and I was helpless to her too. Here lately I could not do shit about anything!

Later that day, after learning the news of Grandma Laura, I laid in bed with the television on and constantly looked over to the spot where I hid my gun. *Is it there or not?* When I heard someone knocking on the front door, wondering who it could be, I turned the television down. I heard the person say, "Its J.J." Mr. J.J was my Aunt Evelyn's husband. I tried my hardest to listen to everything I could when my brother Quick came down into my room to check on me.

I loved my little brothers with all my soul. "Hey Quick come here for a minute," I said, gesturing him over. "Closer fool," with him only a few inches away from me, I whispered, "Quick I'm about to tell you something, and I don't want you to tell anybody else."

Before I could finish my sentence, Quick blurted out, "I already know what you're going to tell me." I was thinking, *can this little fucker read my mind*, when he went on talking, "I know Grandma has cancer." Although I planned to tell my brothers about our grandmother's illness eventually, I didn't call him over for this reason.

"No.... No that's not why I called you. I want you to look over on the top of the air duct vent and rub your hand on top of it and let me know if you see my gun."

"OOOH. You have a gun," he asked curiously.

I smiled, "Quick just hurry up and check before someone comes down here." Doing as I asked Quick ran over to the place; I instructed him to go and rubbed on top the vent and pulled the gun out. While he was removing the gun from the ceiling, our cousin Raw yelled down the basement steps at me.

"Hey Will, you down there homey." Quick became afraid and put the gun back as fast as he pulled it out. Raw came down the basement, walked over to me, and gave me a handshake and a friendly hug.

"Will, you looking a bit rough around the edges," he said.

"Hell yeah!" I replied.

Raw soon pulled out his clippers and razor and tightened me up.13 For the next few minutes, while he cut my hair, Raw and I caught up on old times. I used to see a lot of my cousin when I stayed with our grandmother on Winchester. Thinking about Winchester and my grandma had me wondering, *does he know about her having cancer?* With all the thinking I was doing, I nearly forgot the day was his birthday.

"Happy Birthday big cousin," I yelled at him.

Raw confirmed everything I was thinking, when he said, "It's not a Happy Birthday, Will, cause grandma has cancer, and she is moving here."

"I heard all about it, but where is she at now," I said as Quick left the basement to allow me and Raw to talk.

"We just brought her here. She's upstairs!"

"So that's why Y'all are here? It's to bring grandma to live with us starting today?" I continued by explaining to him how I have been stressed out, but I intentionally left out the part about the suicidal and homicidal thoughts I had been having. I only told him about me being stressed from not being able to walk, and to top it off from grandma dying. He tried to comfort me, but there was no hope of achieving that goal. After about an hour in the basement with me, Mr. J.J came down, not too long after they said their goodbye's and left.

Shortly after they left, Levi and Tucker came downstairs to check on me and carry me upstairs to see Grandma Laura. When I saw her, tears began to roll down my face. Despite all the crying I had done, I still had tears reserved for her; my heart ached deeply.

She looked at me with the love any grandmother would have for their grandchild and said, "Boy don't come up here with all them tears. It could always be worse."

I briefly thought of her words and repeated them in my head; *It could always be worse.* And right then I knew she was right because I could be dead.

"Don't you worry about me, boy. You need to get yourself together so I can get on with my life. I sit around here and worry about you all the time," she continued. As sick as Grandma was, she only thought about my well-being; now that is love. She continued by saying, "Will I want you to watch your friends because I've been having dreams, they're going to kill you in the next block."

Her statement scared me a little because I thought the cancer was already spreading to her brain or something. Maybe, she thought like this because my homey shot me in the back. But I was not sure if she knew the whole story or not, all I could say was, "I'll be ok. You just make sure you get yourself together. I am sure the Lord will bring you through the storm."

Her next words would have shocked the average person but for me, it was like speaking to a brick wall.

"Will I am not afraid to die, how about you?"

She surely was not aware how I have been feeling over the last few months, as I felt like *Biggie Smalls* in his *I'm Ready to Die* song. I was willing to die and was also ready to take the life of some others with me. For the next few hours, I sat there with my grandma, sometimes talking and other times simply sitting in silence.

As time passed and it was later in the evening, it became time for the medical pads covering the wounds on my back to be changed. Levi and Tucker came to me. "Will you ready to go back down to your room and allow your grandmother to get some rest," Levi asked.

I nodded in agreement, turning to my grandmother, "We are gonna get through this ordeal. The Lord don't give us nothing we can't handle."

She looked back at me with her kind eyes, "Will I want you to remember what you told me, for your sake."

After that, they took me back down into the basement, cleaned me up and placed me in the bed for the night. Once finished with me they went to attend to my grandmother and her needs. Days like this made me appreciate my family and their willingness to care for others, all to strengthen the family. Love is the only answer for those in need.

CHAPTER SEVEN: THE SECOND CHANCE

The night of my Cousin Raw's birthday, after talking with Grandma Laura, became a moment forever etched in my mind. It was on this night, after everyone had left and my family had gone to bed, I prayed to my Lord, asking for the strength to walk. I prayed there through the night, tears pouring from me like a flood. I cried a river. My mind kept circling the fact I couldn't walk. I kept thinking about my failure to take my own life—how even in that, I felt powerless.

The main thing on my mind and in my prayers was my grandmother's health. When I say I cried, it's exactly what I did. It was not only pain coming from my mind but also from my heart. The shotgun wounded both my back and opened a wound in my heart, one that would take years to heal. A wound no doctor or specialist had the medication or tools to mend.

It was painful to go through so much at one time and be so young. While lying there talking to the Lord, I thought about how much stress my parents must be going through. My prayers went something like this:

Lord, please take this cancer away from my grandmother. My grandmother did nothing to deserve this. Please Father Almighty, give my parents strength. Lord O' Lord, please give my parents courage to change the things they can change and except the things they cannot change. Along with the wisdom to know the difference.

I prayed to the Lord with all the strength I could muster. It was about the only time I wanted to live within the last few years. I wanted to live for my grandmother. I wanted to walk again; I wanted to help nurture my grandmother back to health. My final words to the Lord that night were:

Lord if you give me strength to walk, I promise, I will not bring havoc on others or cause pain or harm to myself!

Then, I fell asleep. During the night while I slept, I had a dream I was running. While running in my sleep, I felt my legs kick and jolt me physically. Somehow my dream had allowed my legs to move; it was enough of a jerk it woke me out of the dream.

When I woke up, I was afraid to attempt to move my legs, for I had not moved them in two years. And I did not want to believe the Lord had given me the strength to move the bottom portion of my body.

I am not sure now if I was afraid because I would fall or because I had to keep my promise to the Lord of not killing those who had shot me.

For a few moments, I stared at my slim legs and feet, building up the courage to attempt to move them. With my prayer in my head, I started to wave my feet back and forth, then I slowly bent my knees. Just as I thought, the good Lord had allowed me to walk again. MY PRAYER WORKED! I let go, and I LET GOD.

I lay there with so much joy until my soft ass started to tear up again. I told myself once I was strong enough, someone was going to pay. This rage had nowhere to go—it simply sat inside me, burning, waiting. Right now I had to push my revengeful intentions aside. My goal now was to try to get upstairs and show everybody the doctors were all wrong, THEY WERE ALL WRONG! I thought about what they said to me those months I spent in *Montebello Rehabilitation Center.*

"Mr. Carter you will most likely never walk again."

I had repeated those words over and over in my head for two years. First, they told my parents I would not come out of my coma, and they were wrong about that. Now they were wrong about me not being able to walk again.

I looked at the clock, and it read 2:37 am, February 4, 1993. As I sat up, I moved my legs to one side of the bed. Although I possessed the ability to move my legs it remained difficult due to atrophy. Maneuvering my legs so they hung off the side of the bed, I placed my feet on the cold basement floor. Placing all my weight on my legs as I stood, I immediately fell to the floor, but the adrenaline had already started pumping within me. I quickly grabbed any sturdy object by me and pulled myself to my feet and stumbled to the stairs. Falling upon the first few steps my heart was racing with excitement.

Somehow, I managed to get back to my feet and one by one, step by step, I took my time and ascended the stairs, being very careful not to fall backward down them and burst open my wound. Crawling up out of the basement took all the energy I had, similar to when I was shot, having to use all the energy I had to crawl up out of **The Hole**.

When I finally reached the top of those stairs, I instantly thanked the Lord for giving me strength to make it. It was a monumental victory. I thought to myself: *With God all things are possible!*

Stumbling through the kitchen, I turned on the light, staring back down the stairs it felt like it took me 30 to 40 minutes to climb them. My attention shifted to the clock hanging on the kitchen wall—it showed 2:57 am. I realized it had taken me nearly twenty minutes to achieve what I once believed would never be possible again. Either way, I was happy and began walking towards my grandma, I found her sound asleep. Not wishing to bother her, I headed towards the stairs leading to the second floor. I stood at the base of the stairs and looked up them, thinking to myself, *they're only another obstacle to overcome.* Then I started to climb.

From the basement to the second floor took me 50 minutes. I was so exhausted once I finally made it to the bathroom at the top of the stairs I collapsed next to Tucker's bedroom. The noise from my fall woke up everybody as they ran out into the hallway. Upon turning on the light, they found me trying to get up off the floor. I had no words to say at the time, but the ear-to-ear smile said it all.

"How did you get up here," my mom asked. Then she noticed I was moving my legs as I attempted to stand.

Now it was about 3:30 am and everyone was so emotional and happy for me. Grandma Laura woke up to all the commotion going on upstairs and screamed, "What's going on up there this time of morning."

Quick ran downstairs, "Grandma, Will made it all the way upstairs by himself! He's walking again! He walked upstairs all by himself!"

She then yelled out, "Will! Hey Will-Yooooo," in a congratulatory fashion.

Levi helped me to my feet and kissed me on the forehead. When Nick noticed I had bust the wound on my back wide opened, yelling, "His back is bleeding!"

They all watched me walk down the hall as if it were the red carpet. Levi told me to go in their room so he could change my medical pads.

Once in my parent's room, Kayden said, "I never stop praying for you."

"Believe it or not, I never stop praying either," I responded.

"I can't believe it. The doctors said you would be paralyzed for life," Levi commented.

I wanted to say, *fuck them, doctors, because they don't know shit. I knew I had to prove them bitches wrong!* However, if I said I would have been picking my teeth up off the floor. Levi wouldn't have cared less about my back bleeding. Instead of speaking my mind, I simply lay across my parents' bed and allowed Levi change my bandages.

While lying there I thought about the time Tucker broke them stink bombs in their room, and I cracked a smile to myself. I'm like, *got damn I love my father*, as he put the clean bandages on my back. Everyone was amped up, but we all had to get to bed, mother's orders. "Will, sleep in Tucker's room for tonight, and tomorrow we're going down to the hospital," she continued.

"Yes Ma'am," was all I said as I stumbled back down to Tucker's room, just to flop on his bed.

Once everybody went to their rooms to prepare for work or school, I lay there in silence and started thinking. When Tucker came back to his bed, the first thing I said to him was, "Tucker I'm going to kill somebody," as I thought about what I told God that day in the hospital. I continued, "I have nothing but hate in me, I don't want to kill my so-called friends. But somebody's mother is going to be wearing black soon."

"Why do you feel like this bro?" Tucker asked.

"All I can say is nobody understand the road I traveled. They don't understand the operations I went through. They don't understand the pain I had to endure or the headaches my family went through. The misery hasn't stopped here."

"I understand how you feel but..."

Before he could get it out, I cut him off, saying, "Nothing you say will change my mind."

He became upset I was being ignorant and cutting him off. I did not give two flying fucks how anybody felt at this time. Tucker eventually knew it was useless to attempt to change my mind, so he went to sleep.

With the room quiet, I began to think about how I fooled God into giving me my strength back to walk. And how I had promised him I would not cause anybody harm if He let me walk again. Then I fell asleep.

The next morning everybody was up and moving around, but I continued to lay down as I did not get much sleep during the night. Eventually, Tucker woke me up and told me to get out of his bed so he could make up his bed. I agreed and went to move my legs but was unable to. I tried and I tried to make them move but I could not.

Tucker said, "Punk get up so you can go to the hospital."

"I can't move my legs," I said, with what had to be pathetic looking eyes.

"You better get up so I can make my bed and get ready for school," he argued.

With an expressionless face, I looked at him, "I can't walk."

"Are you sure?"

"I swear on Grandma's life!"

Tucker then called my parents to see what was going on with me. Here I was back at ground zero, not being able to take care of myself. My mother asked me what had happened and why I could not walk. I don't know why she asked me; it's not like I knew. But her question did make me think of a saying I always heard church folks say: *The Lord gave, and the Lord has taken away.*

I looked at everyone around me, and I could see in their faces, and they wanted this more than I did. Tucker gave me this look! A look which said only one thing, *I told you never to play with God.* That look confirmed exactly what I was thinking about.

I should not have spoken those words the night before. I should not have spoken those words of hate or allowed those thoughts of causing harm. Now look at me, once again I was stranded. I made God a promise, and I should have held up to it! WOW!

Thursday, February 11, 1993, my parents rolled into Montebello Hospital where my parents and I were greeted in the lobby by my doctor. After Levi had pushed me to a back room, the doctor asked me, "Are you sure you walked last night?"

I gave him the simple, *Fuck You* look while thinking, *how is this cracker going to ask me if I am sure I walked last night? I am crippled, not a dumbass retard.* But once again my parents were present so, "I'm sure about me walking last night," was my response.

After what felt like a pointless conversation, the doctor sent me off to the X-ray room. However, the doctor continued to doubt my miracle walk which was seen in his disbelieving facial features. To try to convince him otherwise, Levi explained everything, describing how I had come up from the basement by climbing two flights of stairs—and had done it at 3:00 am.

The doctor said his usual "OK," bullshit answer and nod, and once again brushed what my parents had told him aside, stating once he had put me on the X-Ray machine, it would determine to him if I walked or not.

I was in the X-Ray room for about twenty-five minutes while the doctors continued to run all sorts of tests on me. And if you have not picked up from my tone, I was damn sick of fucking tests, tests were proving nothing. Once they had run their last test, they sat us in the waiting room and told us to stay there until he came back to us, and of course, we waited another fifteen to twenty minutes or so before they returned.

Upon their return the doctors ensure my parents their tests remained the same, explaining the shotgun blast was too close to my spine causing, permanent paralysis of my legs. They explained pellets from the cartridge remained lodged in my chest and would gradually begin to surface beneath my skin over the course of my life. And when this happened, I would be able to pop them out easily. However, they were completely adamant about their tests and how they showed no signs of me walking or having the ability ever to walk again.

At this point, I had had enough of their test bullshit. With my blood boiling, I said, "How are you gonna tell me I didn't walk last night or won't every have the ability to walk because your test didn't say it?"

My mother immediately attempted to calm me down and told me to let her and Levi talk to the doctors. The doctor said he did not know or understand the reason for me walking last night, and all they could go on were their tests. This news had fucked up my day completely. Everything he said after that sounded like *blah, blah, blah, blah* and so on. Everything he said sounded stupid. I felt like he was a piece of shit to me and if I ever got the opportunity, I would kill his ass. I do not understand why, but for some reason, killing the doctor had become a priority for me. I began to think he wanted me to look like an asshole in front of everyone.

I knew and believed I was a strong man, and it was no doubt I got this attribute from my father. Because of this, I knew and believed I would get myself back to being normal, back to walking again. I kept telling myself, *I will walk again, I will make these bullshit ass doctors into believers.* I knew for sure when I got back to walking, I would be stacking money like Damon or scheming like Keenen Wayans.

When we arrived back home, my grandmother was preparing to leave to have chemotherapy performed. I made sure to give her a kiss before she left out. I had learned over the years any moment could be your last.

Days and even weeks before, I was ready to die, but for some reason, I was now dying to live. Looking at Grandma Laura hop out the door for her therapy changed my outlook on life. If God had given me strength once before, now I was certain He could do it again. This time, when I went before Him, I would make sure my heart remained genuine.

On Sunday, February 21, 1993, three weeks after I had miraculously walked, I lay in my bed thinking and praying. I had been praying and asking God for his forgiveness. Three weeks had passed, and the Lord ignored me and my cries. All of my prayers seemed to go unnoticed.

CHAPTER EIGHT: THE TRUE FORGIVENESS

Lord, please let me walk again. Allow me to have the strength in my legs Lord. I will cause no harm. I will take this whole ordeal as a learning experience. I know Father I wanted to get well. I know you knew my intentions. And yes, I still wanted to go to a funeral and turn to the front row of the deceased's family and unload two guns, one being an automatic weapon and the other a big ass handgun. I know you knew if I ever got hold of my gun I would go out and commit murder. Lord, you knew I would have put my gun behind me while I sat in my wheelchair and killed innocent people. Yes, Lord, you know about all of this. I come to you now with a humble heart. Lord, I have a senior prom this year. Please allow me to graduate. Lord, Father, I've been paralyzed for two years now. I will not ever take your love for granted again.

After that prayer, like many others, I said Amen then went to sleep.

I woke up Monday, February 22, 1993, on my mother's birthday, and it felt like an unusual morning for some reason. On this morning, the Lord had given me the courage and urge to get up and walk. Once out of my groggy state, the Lord allowed me to get up by myself and walk up out of basement. This time, I knew it was truly the Lord's love for me. This time, I took my time and walked into the living room as if I was some high official dignitary.

Entering the living room, Grandma Laura said, "Hey Will, do you see them men out backyard digging my grave?"

Her statement messed me up, because now I could walk for the first time in two years, all she could say was something stupid. I was so caught up in

95

myself I neglected my grandmother's health.

Once I came back to reality and focused back on my grandmother and her health, I listened to her words, "Look! Look! There goes the man in that big 'ol hat and a long trench coat," she continued as she pointed towards the back door which was open.

I looked back at the screen door and saw nothing. I thought about what she was saying, as she was trying to tell me her days on earth were coming to an end. It was like she knew and somewhat welcomed the day of her death, as she did not show any signs of fear. I continued to look at her for several seconds as she gazed upon the back door, thinking to myself *she is such a loving woman.*

I continued up the steps after my stop to talk to Grandma Laura, and as I was going up the steps, my youngest brother Nick was coming down. He noticed I was walking for the second time. Like any other little brother would do when they see their oldest brother walking when they haven't walked in years, he rejoiced! My parents were at work, but my Aunt Evelyn was at our house to aid Grandma Laura until our parents returned from work. When she saw me walking around, she was ecstatic.

The first thing she said was, "Whoa!" She was so shocked she put her hand over her mouth as though she was about to scream. Then the tears started slowly rolling from her eyes. This was a very sad moment for me, having realized my grandmother was so close to death, but all Evelyn could do was hug me and hold me in her arms.

We cried in each other's arms because we were on an emotional roller coaster. We were feeling good, bad, ugly, nice, weak, strong, sane and of course insane. I love my Aunt Evelyn for this moment! There were no words spoken amongst us, but we were able to communicate through our emotions.... Anyway, let me get Y'all back to the story...

Now, when my parents returned home, I was walking into the kitchen and had not seen them enter the house as my back was turned to them. My mother screamed, "Will you're walking again!" She scared the hell out of me. Of course, she didn't hesitate to call my doctor, who told her to bring me in immediately, but she explained she wouldn't be able to get me there until the following day.

With the doctor agreeing to see me at 10:45am the following morning, my mother placed the phone on the receiver and turned her attention to my grandmother lying on her bed in the living room.

Everyone stood and sat around her, once again she says, "Do any of you see them, people, out back digging a hole for me?"

"I hate when she talks like that," my mother responded.

"I'm telling y'all the truth," Grandma Laura continued.

As my grandmother explained to us how she has been seeing people working in the backyard, Levi called me into the dining room so he could change my bandages. After several minutes, Aunt Evelyn stood to leave but not before explaining to my parents about my grandmother's actions throughout the day. Giving my mother a kiss and hug, Aunt Evelyn turned to me and said, "Get well soon Levi Carter III," which was her normal statement to me when she was leaving. I am not sure why she calls me by my entire name. She is simply a strange woman, I guess.

At this point in her treatment, my grandmother was starting to lose her hair and her grip on reality from the chemotherapy. Seeing her made me want to get back into shape so I could help her somehow. But as of now, I was taking it day by day and couldn't rush the Lord's blessing. My father gave me my Percocet and went to accompany my mother and grandmother in the living room. After spending time with grandma, Levi went upstairs to bed. I knew all of this was taking a toll on him and my mom.

As the days went on, I started to progress in my ability to walk. The day I walked up in Montebello Rehabilitation Center, as Grandma Laura would say "I shocked the daylights," out of my doctor. Seeing him, I no longer wanted to hurt or cause him any harm. It was like I was possessed with a newfound hope or joy, as the doctors applauded my strength and determination. One of the most amazing moments of the day came when all the doctors and hospital staff gave me a standing ovation for overcoming what appeared to be an unbeatable trial. When they looked at me, I hoped they understood it was God's work, not mine.

I knew I simply wanted to prove them doctor's wrong. I waited two whole, long years to show them all the technology in the world has nothing on the

Lord and the Lord has the last word in everything.

As their applause came to an end, me being me, I had to end with a show. I looked all around at the faces staring at me and said, "Now can I get an Amen?"

I received back an "Amen," in unison from them all. I bowed and walked away. And with the doctors being proven wrong, getting back into school was next on my agenda to complete. Walbrook Senior High School here I come!

The last time I was at Walbrook, the school was still located at Southwestern High School. Remember, a few years back Walbrook had to be combined with Southwestern High School for a couple of years while the city removed asbestos from the building.

Now it was 1993, and I was on my way back to everybody. This would be my first year spent in the actual building of Walbrook, as it was in Southwestern since 1989. I said to myself, *I am of the class of 1993.* I knew I had taken the longest road to reach this point—a path most couldn't endure—and I understood it would take even more effort to catch up with my classmates.

On Wednesday, February 24, 1993, I entered Walbrook High School. It was not a fast walk by any means. I had this slow limp, but it was a limp which was mixed with a pimp walk. Yeah, I know this sounds crazy, but this was now my walk. At the time, I did not care what kind of walk I had, slow, fast, up, down or sideways. I was fortunate enough to be walking at all. This walk I have now is a blessing from God Himself. This little limp pimp walk I have may look crazy, it may look stupid, but to me, it's nothing more than a testament of what an amazing blessing I had received.

Today is 2-24-93, and I am back. So many of my friends felt sorry for me, but nobody felt sorrier for me than I felt for myself. That was two years of my youthful years down the drain, and there was no way of fishing them back out.

As my parents took all the necessary documents to the main office, I started to see a lot of old faces. There goes my nigga Corey and Midget from around my way! And guess what? They had a bunch of girls with them as usual. With my attention on them, the principal, Mr. Billups approached me.

"Will, welcome back," he said as I turned to face him. "I know you had a long and unwanted journey, but you are the strongest student in my 1993 class. Will if you keep going the way you are, NO WEAPONS FORMED AGAINST YOU SHALL PROSPER."

Those words kept echoing in my mind, and I started to believe the good Lord had been keeping me—for reasons I didn't yet understand. I know people who were shot like I was, but the major difference is—they didn't make it.

I looked at Midget and Corey leaning up against the wall fooling around with the girls; I looked again and saw K'mar with them. It's been two years since I saw any of my niggaz. I forgave him and Nelson only because God had forgiven me! I said goodbyes to my parents and started my journey of my first day back in school.

As I walked down the school hallways, one would have thought I was floating, as all the staff and students stared at me like I was some ghost which had returned from the underworld to take vengeance upon them. Well, if that's what they were thinking, they were pretty close to being right. I did go to the far limit of life, where life and death are only separated by a line as thin as a hair. Yeah, I was there, and I looked death in the eye and, fortunately, with divine help was able to turn my back to it.

Everyone continued to look at me as I hopped my way down the hall to my 12th-grade class, taught by Mrs. Topaz, my home tutor, and the greatest teacher ever. Entering the class, no one knew I had taken the home tutorial and was up in the current studies. She demanded I learn and work hard while I was home, and she was right, as for this year it all paid off. I had all the credits I needed to get into the 12th grade.

Being the fool, naturally I stepped into the class saying, "So here I am, back from the grave!" All eyes turned to face me standing in the classroom doorway. It was one of the great memories in life I can never repeat. All the girls came over to see what was up with me, and to be honest I think most of them were turned on because I had survived a shooting. You know these hood chicks love gangsta shit.

Here I was, one of the earliest shootings ever in Walbrook's Senior High School history. I had all the basic classes like English, Social Studies, Business Economics, and Gym, which of course I could not do so well in, due to prior events. And finally, I had lunch. Yeah, it was not technically considered a class by the Board of Education; however, to me, it was because once upon a time I had to learn how to eat all over again.

It was March 1993, and I only had three months left, and I would be finished with this school thing. However, it would prove a difficult month at Walbrook, for all my niggaz from around my neighborhood were beefing with gangstas from The Junction or the Popular Grove areas. I was starting to hang with my niggaz, and they were representing Edmondson Avenue, also known as E.A. But they were raised up on Appleton and Riggs, known as **The Hole**.

It was kind of awkward at first to be back in the midst of the people I thought originally wanted me dead. I had gained so much street credit with the dudes from E.A. because I never once snitched on nobody. That alone had people wanting to be my friends, as there is honor amongst G's. As I hung out more and more with them, I started to look at these guys like true friends. I believe what happened to me in the basement could have just as easily happened to either of us. Of course, we were young and dumb, although being young and dumb almost made me pay the ultimate price.

What's amazing is I've never truly thought about what I'm about to say, and I've never shared these words with anyone before. I wonder—if I had been the one who shot one of them that night, would they have been as loyal to me as I was to them? I often think about this now, but since I never put a gun to them, all I can do is put those thoughts on the backburner.

The majority of my friends by this time had started selling dope on Edmondson Avenue and Pulaski Street. But since I was gone so long, so much had changed, and my friends were no exception. Only years ago, we were stealing clothes off people's lines because we could not afford them ourselves. Now my friends had diamonds on their necks and wrist. They all had what we used to call 'Dopeboy Money.' Dopeboy Money meant someone had at least five to six thousand dollars in their pocket at any given moment.

Midget used to take time out of his busy schedule in school to make sure I was good with anything, money, food, etc. I do not know if he thought he owed me or had to return a favor since I did not snitch on anyone about the shooting in the basement. There were times Midget came to the class and would buy the entire class lunch, and there were, at least, fifteen people in my class. Midget was drowning in cash, and he was still just a high school kid. Word got around fast, and suddenly every girl wanted to be close to him—real close. It wasn't just about him; it was about the lifestyle, the money, the shine. They were lining up to offer a taste, hoping to get a taste in return. Midget knew so many girls it put many of us to shame. They would simply become the usual whores around the neighborhood. I call them hoes because they wanted nothing else but the money.

It didn't take long before the neighborhood conflicts my friends were involved in began spilling over into the classroom. One day, a guy from the Junction ran into my classroom and popped the shit out one of my homies, landing the punch right across his cheekbone. And if my boy did not know how to take a hit, his ass would have been laying there on the floor knocked the fuck out.

Although I could not walk well, I had the heart of a lion, but during this time, I did not give two shits about fighting with anybody. Even though I used to carry a reputation for not giving a fuck, I guess sitting in bed for two years is enough to change anyone's ways. However, the real reason I wanted to stop fighting was because I had made a promise to God. I had to keep this promise because he controlled everything, and I knew this from experience. The last time I backed out on a promise, I woke up the following morning unable to walk. The thought of this alone kept me on the straight and narrow—at least for a while.

One day Midget told me he knew somebody who was selling turntables and not your old grandma wooden box turntables, but the best turntables you could find on the streets.18 He described them as being twelve hundreds. Yeah, you heard me, twelve hundreds, and during the 1990s, these were considered the top end. Well, on this particular day Midget was telling me about the turntables, and he asked me to leave school with him and pick them up.

Huh, can you say fucking Déjà vu? The last time I decided to cut school with this fella, I got shot in his basement by his little brother Nelson. That mistake cost me two years of my life. And now he had the nerve to ask me to leave with him again. Everything seemed as though it was coming back full circle. But I was at a point in my life where I figured nothing walking the face of the earth could scare me except the spiritual world and God. I say the spiritual because I figured if someone touched you wrong physically, you could always retaliate, but not with spirits.

Anyway, I finally decided to leave school early with Midget to get the turntables he told me about. About a half hour later we had the turntables with no issues and had them back at my house. Without any hesitation I started messing around with them, trying my best to mix me a few tracks here and there. And hey, what can I say, I was a natural at it. And honestly, Midget saw something in me I had never seen before. I never saw myself being a DJ, but Midget did, and he instantly gave me the name D.J Blackbird as I did my thing on the turntable. Cutting school on this particular day was well worth it.

My life was taking a drastic turn for the better, and with a great life came the girls. Out of nowhere, I found myself tangled up with more women than I could count—enough to bruise Hugh Hefner's pride if he'd been watching. It was like I had been rocketed into Walbrook High School stardom. Girls would literally go down on me if I told them about my hospital experience, No Bullshit. There is something about a street nigga that turns them on! Whatever I did from now on had to be the best.

But when good things come, believe me when I say the bad is closely following. Not too long after getting the turntables, one of my homies shot up a McDonald's located in the Junction to get at one of the guys from a rival gang. Sadly, he missed his target and killed a little girl.

That little girl dying brought back so many memories; it was like being hit by a freight truck. The Life, The Struggle, **The Hole**. I can go on and on talking about my pain, my suffering, my headache, my loneliness, my doubt and my fear of dying. But this is little in comparison to what happened to the little girl; she never saw it coming! She was released from school that day, like many of us, and before she was shot, the day seemed typical. A typical day which was ended by the eruption of a 9mm, whose rounds had hit the girl in the back of the head, ending her life instantly. I never knew the girl's name, only her was shown on the news.

When I came back to school the following day, my dudes were in a full out war. The little girl who was killed the day before was probably related to one of the guys my homies were beefing with, as simple fights escalated into all-out wars in the streets. Things got so bad random guys walked into classrooms and started strangling people—it was unlike anything I had ever seen before.

Once my father got news of this epic gang crime taking place in and near my school (it was all over the news), he became worried I was involved because of my own friend's behaviors. At the time, I saw this as perfect timing for me because it was my senior year. I figured even with my limp walk; I was not going to let anyone beat me down because of my homie's actions. So, I started carrying a .38 special handgun with me to school in my backpack. I was not going to go down without a fight. I was not going down again.

My pops, Levi, had the streets wired into his bones—there wasn't a move made he didn't feel coming. So when my crew started wildin' out, he didn't lecture me. He made a power play. Levi pulled up with a candy apple red 300ZX, gleaming like sin under the sun. Chrome BBS wheels, T-top roof, manual transmission—pure heat. That car wasn't just a ride; it was a statement. But it came with a catch: I had to learn the clutch. Took me damn near a week to tame that five-speed beast, stalling out more times than I care to admit. But once I got it, I was gone.

When I rolled up to Walbrook in that candy red 300ZX, everything changed. Heads turned, doors opened, hearts, and yeah—chicks legs. That car wasn't just a ride, it was a magnet. The attention was wild, and the energy? Electric. I won't lie, it felt like I'd leveled up overnight. Later on, I found out my pops had deeper reasons for putting me behind that wheel. Levi didn't want me standing around outside the school, waiting on the bus, where fights broke out and bullets didn't ask questions. That car was his way of keeping me moving—literally and figuratively—out of harm's way

In 1993, Walbrook was out of control with the fighting, shootings and all the students thinking they were the slickest. Sometimes, I would look around at the stupidity and started not to give a fuck again as I witnessed the nonsense every day. I was like, none of these niggaz ever witnessed a murder. None of them ever witnessed death. Not one of them experienced the pain I did to get back here. I lost countless pints of blood, sweat, and tears. And simply writing this, I feel myself becoming very emotional. So, I will stop here....No! No! No! I am kidding. I cannot stop. I must tell my story, so I will continue writing.

With time, my homies beefed more and more against rival neighborhood gangs; it was like a scene out of *Colors*. And as much as I thought I wanted to be a part of it and have my boys back, the beefing shit was simply too heavy for one thing. And secondly, my body would not allow me.

While my friends were outside selling drugs, making dough, I was in the house improving my skills on my turntables. Day in and day out, my father began to take notice of my skills and as my passion for music increased, he brought me speakers, an amplifier and a couple of albums to get started. My discovery of mixing was a blessing in disguise, as it kept me off the streets and out of danger. I started to spend hours upon hours in the house playing on my 1200s. And when I did go outside to hang with my niggaz, I made sure to put my gun in my dip. I never knew what those niggas would be into.

My *SIG 9mm* held sixteen rounds, plus one in the chamber, and she was nothing to play with. I kept thinking whatever came my way and meant me harm, I would start shooting, no questions asked! I figured when it came to me carrying a gun, I'd rather get caught with it than to get caught without it. I would rather be tried by twelve jurors than to be carried by six pallbearers.

Truth be told, I was terrified of getting shot again. I was not scared of hanging out with my boys; I was only worried because of my thought of that little girl was shot not so long ago. And the shit was still on my mind. I could not help but wonder, *what if something like that happened to me*, especially with me overcoming my recent trials.

Although they sold drugs, were constantly beefing with other gangs, always evading the cops, and regularly keeping an eye out for the stick-up-boys, my homies were still nice guys in my book.

The street life was like a concrete jungle, and it had all kinds of animals. OOPS! I meant all kinds of people, who simply did not give a shit. And because of this, I started hanging with my brothers and family a lot more. I even learned how to cut hair as a pastime, and my brothers acted as my clients.

Needless to say, my father did not mind me cutting their hair either, as it saved money from coming out of his pocket with having to send us to the barber shop. Like many other things, cutting hair had come naturally, I had become so good at it other friends and family would come from all over the city to have me cut their hair.

Many of my friends and family came and sat in a chair before me to have their hair cut. But there is one individual who sat before me that I would never forget, and that was Uncle Yancy. Yeah, you may laugh and chuckle at the name, but do not get it twisted. Uncle Yancy was an Ol' G from top to bottom. He was one of those cool uncles, you know. One of the people who always had positive things to say and kept a smile on your face. But if need be, was ready to step up to any scenario and handle his business, if you were to approach him the wrong way.

Well, one day my Uncle Yancy, who was the best friend of my father, came over to get his hair cut and brought my cousins Murphy and Orenda. Just like any other time I saw him, he greeted me and told me how strong I was to overcome what I had gone through and how I should use my second chance to do something special in life. In honest truth, he was a good, Goodman. He was a real man and a real father. On this particular day, after I cut his hair, he gave me $5.00 as usual and told my father that he would talk to him soon.

Later on, in the evening my father received a call and was told Yancy had been killed in his car. My father never talked to Uncle Yancy again.

The authorities believed one of Yancy's friends had him killed or had killed him themselves. This incident completely blew my mind, for he was only sitting in front of me hours before. His untimely end illustrated to me how fast death could sneak up on anyone.

About a week later we went to view Uncle Yancy's body; it was as though I had cut Yancy's hair for his funeral. And it was at his funeral in which I saw my father cry for the second time, the first time being when I was shot.

Yancy's untimely death was an eye opener for me concerning the street life. The street life was harsh. The street life ended the lives of many, even the innocent. The street life turned friends to foes. It would have you believing your friends were true friends, but instead they were secretly your enemies.

And when your friends were secretly your enemies, we labeled those guys *frienemies*. The streets would have sons selling their mothers crack cocaine. The streets would have brothers plotting on one another. Now that I think about it, what positives could be told about the street life?

When we hear about these different scenarios on the news, we tend to ignore the matter as a people. And it is not because we are ignorant, it is because the media helps to desensitize us to it through movies and television. However, the illusion is portrayed on television is much different than folks are aware of, and they only learn of this once tragedy strikes home. The street is called the concrete jungle, and corrupt is one of the only words which comes to mind when I think of it. **The Hole** comes to mind when I think of it!

When I first got word of Yancy being killed by one of his friends, it had me wondering about my friends. I believed that I got shot behind negligence. But unfortunately, the saying goes: *Keep you friends close and your enemies closer.*

Yancy's was the second funeral I had ever attended, with Reverend Odenton's being the first. I learned the hard way—there's a huge difference between losing someone close through violence and losing them to natural causes. That difference was the desire for revenge.

CHAPTER NINE: THE MOURNING

Days were passing, and I truly did not know how to mourn over my Uncle Yancy, as crying was not doing a damn thing. I figured driving around might help me forget about him, but it didn't help either. While driving around, I stumbled across a girl selling reefer at the gas station on Monroe and Lafayette. I bought two dime-bags which were $10 per bag. Afterwards, I went to the liquor store and purchased two Dutch Masters, a pint of Hennessy and a bottle of water.

I figured I was going to bury this feeling one way or another, so why not feel good doing it? Before I left the parking spot in front of the liquor store, I rolled up both blunts. With my blunts rolled I pulled off bumping to *'Back Down Memory Lane'* by *Minnie Riperton*. You may call me soft, but I did not care. As I drove down Monroe Street, I sparked up my first blunt and let the smoke fill my lungs.

I had never smoked marijuana before, but I had to ease my mind about Yancy. I poured me a small shot of Henny while I hit Route 295 South. As I started feeling the substance I was taking in, I began to sing, "Back down memory lane, save me, save me," while driving on that beautiful spring night.

Halfway through the blunt, I started geeking by looking in the mirror making funny faces at myself. I got off on the exit onto Nursery Road. I did not think about where I was going; I was simply enjoying the spring air and putting my mind at ease. I took off the T-top from the 300ZX and turned up the music volume. My mood had changed from Minnie Riperton to wanting to bump some N.W.A. Popping in the cassette tape, all I heard was Easy-E, "What the Fuck is up....in the place to be.... Rockin on the mic.... it's Easy Mutha Fuckin

E."

Ok...Ok...Ok I was feeling the effect of the reefer. It did its job and took my mind completely off Yancy. I only smoked one blunt, but my tolerance level was low and nowhere near some of my friends. The blunt combined with the liquor had me in a zone I had never been in before. If the police had pulled me over, they would have most likely taken my funny looking ass straight to jail for the night.

Eventually, I came to a stop sign, so I slowly brought the car to a stop. I waited and waited. I sat at the stop sign damn near ten minutes waiting for the stop sign to turn green. Once I realized what the hell, I was doing I started to laugh uncontrollably at my foolishness. I laughed so hard my face started to hurt, and I tried to stop but I could not.

The crazy thing about it was I knew I had nothing to laugh at. After laughing nearly forty-five minutes, I figured it was perpetual. Sitting there in my laughing state I received a beep on my pager, and it read: CODE #2. I immediately knew it was one of my brothers because they were the only ones to use this code, my parents used CODE #1.

Getting myself together, I drove to the nearest gas station and called the number back. The phone rang once, and Tucker picked up quick.

"Hello."

"Yo Tucker what's up?"

"Hey, Will the police just raided Rue's house. I was hoping you weren't in there."

As serious as the situation was, my dumb ass continued to laugh.

"Why are you laughing so hard and about what?" he asked.

I never did answer his question, I simply told him, "I'm cool. I'll be back shortly." Hanging up the phone, I looked down at my hands and noticed they were shaking. I instantly and oddly became nervous, thinking the police were going to pull me over. My mind switched to the weed and how toxic it had to be, and how the girl at the gas station must have been attempting to kill me. I panicked. I started to pray to God, "God, please bring me down off this high and I will never smoke again."

Turning down N.W.A as the gangsta rap was not aiding my emotions at the moment. I couldn't remember any of my friends acting like *this* after smoking reefer. All my senses appeared to be heightened as I could hear my heart beating, but through all this, I continued to laugh. Swapping cassette tapes again, I popped in the gospel song *'Rough Side of the Mountain by F.C. Barnes'* my mom had left in the car.

I had no clue why in the hell I was listening to gospel music. I guess it was to stop me from laughing. After twenty more minutes, I started to come down from the high an hour and a half from the moment I started smoking. I was not going to go back around my way geeking like this, so I drove a little longer around by the airport before I headed back into town.

On my way back into town I started to think really heavy again, being I was coming down off my high. My mind meandered its way to thinking about Grandma Laura and how she was very sick and how the therapy was not working. As a result, she was talking more and more about death. Hearing the words to the song, "Rough Side of The Mountain" I started to follow along,

"This old race will soon be over, and there will be no more race for me to run Lord. But I got to stand before God's throne, and all my heartache will be gone. I can hear my Savior say, 'Welcome Home.'"

I was thinking, *is this how Grandma was feeling? Were these words written for my grandmother? Can people who are dying know their date of Death? How will I be if she goes before me?* All these questions flooded into my mind at once. I still had one blunt left, but I refused to smoke it. I knew how the Lord worked with me making promises. If I promised Him or made an agreement with Him, he expected me to keep it.

As my high began to fade, I reflected on the moment I promised the Lord—if He let me walk again, I wouldn't seek revenge for being shot. When he gave me what I wanted, I still kept the revenge and hate in me. The Lord had paralyzed me another three to four weeks. Believe me; I learned my lesson with playing with God. Therefore, the last blunt stayed where it was.

Turning left from Fulton Avenue and onto Riggs Avenue, I got caught at the next traffic light. I saw a crowd of people looking over at my man Rue's house as they watched the police raiding his place. The light turned green, and I pulled off, continuing to make my way down Riggs, then a right onto the 1100 block of Appleton Street, **The Hole**.

As high as I was, I still went into the living room and chilled with my grandmother. I told her I loved her and how I did not want her to leave me.

She looked at me and said, "Will, ard, hush boy, I'm not going anywhere." And as confident as she sounded, I still knew and understood her days were numbered.

CHAPTER TEN: THE FRIENDS

It was Saturday, May 15, 1993, and Aunt Peggy, Midget's mother, moved off of Riggs Avenue and around the corner onto Monroe Street. Since hanging with Midget and Nelson every day since I moved into **The Hole,** I had been calling Ms. Peggy my aunt. Rue told me they moved around on Monroe Street because the landlord on Riggs refused to make any repairs to the house. Honestly, Ms. Peggy should've moved as soon as I got shot in the goddamn basement!

Their house on Riggs Avenue stayed empty for a month before someone else moved in! And if I gave you three chances to guess who moved in Aunt Peggy's old house, you would never guess correctly. So, don't bother trying to figure out who moved in. I am going to tell you who it was! It was my other grandmother, Inas. She had to move into the same damn house I got shot in. Along with Grandma Inas, my Uncle Melvin, and my two Aunts Faith and Regina moved in with her.

Not long after, Grandma Inas began coming around **The Hole** to look after Grandma Laura while my parents kept working. Being this close to both my grandmothers reminded me of the days spent on Stricker and Winchester Streets. We had nearly the entire family in the neighborhood. Next door to us was Aunt B. and all of our crazy cousins. Around on Riggs Avenue were Grandma Inas and some of my crazy aunts and uncles. Since we moved down in **The Hole** in 1988 so much had occurred.

With the end of the school year near, I got me a summer job at my Aunt Evelyn's job. There, I would be working as an animal caretaker at {G.R.C.} Gerontology Research Center, which was located at the *Francis Scott Key Medical Hospital, now it's known as John Hopkins Bayview Medical*. It was my first serious job—and a federal one too—where my only responsibility was cleaning all the animal and mice cages. The good thing about it was they paid me $14.10 an hour, and this was back in 1993.

Some of the cages I was responsible for included the dog kennels and pig pens. I had to make sure to scrape up the poop then spray the kennels down with a hot power hose. Cleaning the pig pen was similar to the dog kennel except I had to throw hay down after power washing.

For the mice and white rats, I had to scrape and clean their cages, find the ones that had died from various experiments, and dispose of their bodies. It may seem like a lot of work, but it wasn't, since I had help, which made the job much easier.

While I was spending the majority of my day working, my brothers, Tucker, and Quick, started hanging with a bunch of little dudes from **The Hole** and other nearby blocks, and they formed *The Lynch Mob Crew*. To entertain themselves, they ran around beating up anyone they could—especially those who didn't live in the neighborhood. And if you were a drunk, I felt sorry for you, as you would have been the first to get the beat down. To put it simply, they were some bad ass kids, and there was maybe a total of thirty of them.

It was not too long after our cousin Bruce joined *The Lynch Mob Crew*. These little bad ass guys terrorized the neighborhood. It was a guarantee any kid who would come through our hood and did not belong would not be walking back out of our hood. One time, the Lynch Mob cornered a kid—beat him within an inch of his life, then carved him up with shards from shattered bottles. This is one example of the cruel things these little monsters did to their victims.

June '93 hit, and I finally crossed that stage—high school in the rearview, after one hell of a ride. Summer came in hot, and Cappuccino's was lit like never before. The spot had turned legendary, and with that came a different kind of attention. Girls started showing up, not just for the vibe, but for what the clubhouse had come to represent—status, allure, danger wrapped in velvet. It wasn't just about the sheets and pillows anymore. We had heat in the stash too. The whole setup had evolved—comfort, chaos, and clout, all under one roof.

I remember K'mar had this girl, Michelle, over at the spot. I got bored and slid in—figured she'd hesitate, but she grabbed me like she'd been waiting. K'mar was behind her, I was getting mine up front. Just as we were about to switch, Test came strolling in like it was nothing. She was completely bare, but didn't flinch when someone walked in. K'mar kept going like nothing changed. It wasn't until Test stood over us that she finally pulled away from me—just for a moment.

"Bitch I'm Next!" Test eventually said.

"What? I don't even get down like that," she responded, fixing her hair.

"Girl, you let them two fuck your ass. Now your dumb ass is gonna let me hit it, damn dummy."

She gave him that look—like he was talking nonsense, and she wasn't buying a word of it. I was thinking, *For Test wanting to get some coochie he surely is not trying to sweet talk the girl.*

"I'm not giving you a damn thing. And for your damn information I didn't fuck Will," she yelled.

I guess all the yelling finally threw K'mar off—he stopped mid-stroke. Yeah, you heard that right. He was still going while Michelle was full-on arguing with Test. Wild, I know. But that's just how things played out back then.

Anyway, Michelle—still stark naked—kept arguing with Test like nothing else mattered. Then he did what had sadly become routine for him: pulled a gun on her. K'mar didn't waste a second—he jumped out of bed and started throwing on clothes. Michelle wasn't even eighteen, and now she had a barrel aimed at her face just because she wouldn't give it up. Maybe she was fed up, maybe she thought he was bluffing—but she stood up, bare as ever, and started dressing like she'd made her decision.

"Bitch what the Hell you doing. What I asked you to do was come over here, bend dat ass over and let me do my thing," said Test, holding the gun tilted sideways. But she continued ignoring this while she pulled down her shirt.

It was chaos unfolding, but I couldn't take my eyes off her—she was stunning. Skin smooth like caramel, short hair styled in tight finger waves, and a body that didn't need help turning heads. Her chest was firm, standing proud without a bra, and that bubble in the back was something else. She smelled fresh, clean, everything groomed just how I liked. And the way she stood there, unfazed with a gun in her face? That told me she'd been around dealers before—this wasn't her first time staring down madness

"This hoe acting like she doesn't understand my ass. Bitch I said bend your ass over," Test continued, the frustration building in him as it was written on his face.

"Test chill man," I said, trying to calm him down. K'mar was on the side laughing his ass off.

As Michelle reached for her pants, Test fired—no hesitation. The bullet tore clean through the fabric, leaving a smoking hole where her hand had just been.

"What the fuck. Nigga are you crazy or......." Before she could finish her statement, a shot rang out right above her head. Her eyes went bug-eyed as she pulled back from them. If she hadn't known he was serious before, she definitely knew now.

"Ok. Ok, I'll give you some," she said as she pulled up her shirt and bent over for Test to hit.

"I thought you would see it my way," he said, as he eased in and started to hit it from the back. His gun pointed to the back of her head.

I was ready to dip by now because I'm now thinking this is rape, but for some reason, this girl's body had me mesmerized.

"Now ain't this better? Why did you do all that fussing when all you had to do is this? If you ever come in my house to fuck somebody, then, believe me, you gonna have to fuck me also," Test continued, not missing a stride in his stroke. I just kept hoping the gun wouldn't go off by accident and turn the room into a crime scene. But then she started to moan—maybe it was fear, maybe something else. Either way, it seemed like she'd grown used to Test's brand of chaos, "Ho shut the Hell up and take it."

Not long after he finished, he yanked up his pants, grabbed her clothes, and bolted out of the clubhouse. I felt a weight settle in my chest. I kept asking myself—was I just as guilty for standing by? What she did with me was consensual, but that wouldn't stop her from telling the cops otherwise. She tried to clean herself up, but the damage was already done. Tears streamed down her face as she screamed at K'mar—she came with him, and he should've protected her. I didn't know what to say. She'd been violated, and now all we could do was watch her break.

Naked, she paced the trailer floor, back and forth, lost in thought. Probably trying to figure out her next move. If I were in her shoes, my mind would be racing too—trying to make sense of what just happened, what comes next, and how the hell to escape it all. *Do I tell my people, should I tell anyone, and if I do what will happen to me?*

Whatever was running through her mind, I couldn't look away. Her body was unreal—curves that demanded attention, and a chest that held its own without effort.

She started yelling, voice cracking with rage and disbelief. "How the hell did y'all let him rape me right in front of you? He shot at my clothes, nearly blew my head off. I must be some kind of damn fool for even having sex in a trailer," she said, collapsing onto the bed. Then she turned to me, eyes burning. "I gave you head and don't even know your name. What's your damn name, anyway?"

The first thing came out of my mouth was, "Fuck that, you ain't telling the police I did this to you."

"I ain't gonna tell the police on you. It will make me feel better knowing your name."

"Hell, you just sucked me off, and I never got your name."

"Well, you never asked," she said, flashing a faint smile. I thought to myself—when could she have told me, anyway? Her mouth was full, and she was moaning while K'mar handled his business behind her. "Just call me a dummy," she added, "like your boy did."

"Ok dummy," I said with a smile. "How your tail getting home with no clothes?"

"She's gonna have to stay here with you while I grab her some clothes," K'mar said, eyes locked on Michelle. "But first, I need to find out where Test ran off to." Before either of us could respond, he bolted out of the trailer, leaving me alone with her in the thick silence.

With everyone gone, the trailer fell into a heavy silence. Just me and her, locked in a moment that felt too long. She looked at me, I looked back—neither of us saying a word. The quiet was suffocating, so I broke it. "Now that it's just us," I said, "why don't you come give me a little something?"

"No," she said quickly, but something in her tone didn't match the word. I moved closer, sat beside her, unsure but drawn in. I reached out gently, testing the moment. She didn't pull away. Didn't say another word. The silence hung heavy, but her stillness spoke louder than anything.

"Your ass love sex, don't you?"

"What you think?"

"I think you're gonna put this condom on me with your mouth."

"Ok. But if we are going to do this, we need to do it before K'mar gets back," she whispered softly as she nibbled on my ear.

In my head, it was game time. I knew K'mar wouldn't be back anytime soon—he had to track down Test. That gave me space, and I soaked up every second of it. She was a dime, no doubt. When she slid the condom on with her lips, I knew it was on. From the wall to the floor, side to top, she matched every move I threw at her. It felt less like sex and more like a full-blown rodeo—wild, relentless, and unforgettable.

"Let off in my mouth," she moaned.

She said something that cracked open my brain—sharp, unexpected, like a match struck in the dark. I didn't hesitate. I followed her lead, caught in the gravity of her confidence. I was sixteen, still figuring out the edges of myself, and she moved like someone who'd long since mapped her own terrain. There was no fumbling, no second-guessing—just intention. She taught me something I hadn't known I was ready to learn. After her, every encounter carried a trace of that moment—an imprint.

I went at her like I had something to prove, like time didn't exist. But when I finally collapsed beside her, she didn't stop. She leaned back, legs up against

CHAPTER TEN: THE FRIENDS

the wall, chasing something I hadn't given her. Maybe I hadn't hit the mark. Maybe she just needed more than I could offer. She was wild and brilliant and reckless in equal measure. A storm wrapped in skin. And I was just trying to hold on long enough to understand what the hell had just happened.

After what Test did, I figured my chances were shot. But once I got mine, I was ready to bounce. If K'mar didn't show up in the next ten minutes, I was out—leaving her behind in that trailer, no second thoughts.

Just as I was getting ready to head out, she snapped, "You ain't seriously leaving me here alone. I hear somebody else coming."

"Oh, shit them my boys coming."

"If they are your boys. I'm not having sex anymore," she said pulling her knees up to her chest in a fetal position. I guess her shop was closed.

Midget, Corey, Rue, and Nelson came up in the trailer. Seeing me with this bomb chick the first thing they asked me was, "Are you sharing?" I told them what Test had done, and they immediately burst into laughter.

Rue sank into the chair and laid it all out—the cops had raided his spot and found 106 grams of heroin stashed in his room. Since it was in his space, he took the fall. No one else got cuffed. Just him

"Yo I'm out on a $80,000 bail, so my niggas, I'm about to hit the block hard so I can save up this $10,000 for this lawyer," Rue continued.

While Rue was breaking down the raid—how the cops hit his spot and found the heroin—Nelson, wild as ever, did something reckless. He whipped it out and started pressing Michelle for a favor. He kept at it for a few minutes, talking slick, until K'mar finally showed up with her clothes. Turns out he couldn't find Test anywhere, so he hit Mondawmin Mall and bought her a whole new outfit. Dropped $250 on top of that. Then, trying to clean up the mess Test left behind, he apologized and asked her to keep quiet about everything that went down. She agreed. Now whether she agreed because of how I handled things—or because she was stuck in a trailer full of wild, thirsty dudes—I couldn't say for sure.

The crazy thing about the entire situation was that after K'mar had given her the money, my crazy ass friends tried to rob the girl of it. With all that went down and her agreeing to keep her mouth closed, K'mar and I did not allow them to. But it was still pretty damn funny.

   She slipped the cash into her pocket, got dressed, and walked out with K'mar. That was the last time I saw Michelle. Shame, really. Would've been nice to run that back a few more times. Maybe she moved out the neighborhood, or maybe K'mar kept seeing her on the low and just never said a word. Either way, wherever that girl ended up, she stuck in my memory.

CHAPTER ELEVEN: THE SUMMER OF 1993

By July 4th, '93, summer was in full swing, and there was only one place to be—the Inner Harbor. Tradition ran deep, so the crew and I headed downtown like we always did, posted up to catch the fireworks lighting up the sky. But the night didn't stay peaceful for long. Corey clocked a few heads from Walbrook Junction in the crowd, and once he pointed them out, things escalated fast. Nelson didn't hesitate—walked straight up, cracked one in the face, then spun and dropped another with a blindside to the jaw. Just like that, chaos erupted. Fireworks overhead, fists flying below. The crowd scattered, screams mixing with explosions. Me? I stayed back. Fighting wasn't my lane—not then, not ever.

I had my piece on me, and when things started spiraling, I made a split-second decision to shut it down fast. I pulled it, let off shots at niggaz, and the crowd erupted—panic everywhere, bodies pushing and shoving to get clear. This was Baltimore, after all. I should've known better. Out here, nearly everyone's carrying. Sure enough, one of the dudes reached for his own—a Tech-9, heavy and loud.

It did not take long before it started roaring, BOOM! BOOM! POW! POW! Two people instantly dropped to the ground from a bullet to the head, their brains laying on the pavement. Of course, I felt sorry for whomever they were, but I also did not want to be homeboy's next victim either, so I got up out of there.

Cops swarmed in from every angle, trying to lock down the scene and figure out who'd been firing. But with the crowd packed tight and chaos still rippling through the Harbor, it was a lost cause. The shooters had already melted into the masses, and back then, there weren't cameras on every corner like there are now. It was like chasing shadows in a thunderstorm—needle in a haystack kind of impossible.

Truth be told, I was relieved we didn't get caught that night. The cops flooded the scene, but everyone who mattered slipped through the cracks—including the guys who'd come at us. They got away from the law, but not from us.

The next evening, around 9 p.m., we rented a car and headed up to Walbrook Junction. It didn't take long to spot them—same crew from the Harbor, posted on a corner, surrounded by a bunch of teenagers, heads down, unaware. They weren't watching their backs, and in a city like Baltimore, that's a dangerous game to play.

My boys rolled up, windows down, and let the steel speak. The corner lit up. By the end of it, the two who'd fired on us the night before were gone. July 5, 1993—that was the day the score got settled.

I was caught between fear and grit—tough on the outside, but adrenaline had me wired. My heart was thumping like a drumline. I didn't want to get caught, not for this. I was behind the wheel, not just because they said I was the best driver, but probably because I was the only one with a legit license. That made me the default. For days afterward, I couldn't shake the paranoia. I kept replaying the scene, wondering if someone had clocked our faces or remembered the rental. Every glance felt like a question. Every silence, a threat.

If it isn't obvious by now, I broke the promise I made to God. I knew it the moment I crossed that line, and the weight of it settled heavy on my chest. I kept wondering how He'd deal with me—how the punishment would come. The Lord sees everything, that much I believe. But part of me hoped maybe, just maybe, He'd looked away this once. Still, even if His gaze had shifted, the truth doesn't change: every wrong carries its price. And I knew mine was coming.

After ending those guys lives, I could not help but ponder about how I cheated death myself, which sort of made me feel invincible. And because of my feelings of invincibility, I took on the principle, *"Show No Love Because Love Will Get You Killed."*

I tried to justify my actions to the Lord. He had to understand why I did the things I did, for He created me. I wasn't looking for trouble, but trouble always found me. This was what I wanted God to understand. He had to understand, the struggle, the pain, **THE HOLE**!

The next morning, I had to be at work by 8:30. Rain was coming down steady, slicking the roads with that quiet kind of danger. I was behind the wheel of my 300ZX, but my mind wasn't in the driver's seat—it had drifted off, lost in a daydream about my wild godfather, Chey.

One second I was laughing to myself, the next I was sliding. I lost control. The tires gave out, and before I could react, I was under the belly of a semi-truck. Metal crunched, glass shattered, and just like that, my candy red ride was gone—totaled. All because I wasn't watching the road. Just watching memories.

Chey was one of my father's closest friends—loyal, wild, and always around. But he battled a heavy drinking problem that often took him down dark roads. One night, caught in the haze of a binge, he ended up with someone who was living with HIV. That one decision changed everything. Not long after, Chey tested positive. Within two weeks, the virus had progressed to full-blown AIDS. His decline was fast, and brutal. It wasn't long before we lost him.

Losing Chey cut deep—straight to the bone. After he passed, not a day went by that I didn't think about him. That morning, his memory was heavy on my mind, pressing down like the rain that had started to fall. I was behind the wheel, but my head was somewhere else, tangled in thoughts of my godfather and everything we'd lost.

By the time I snapped back to the moment, it was already too late. The light had turned red, and a tractor-trailer was barreling through the intersection. I never saw it coming until it was right there—unstoppable.

There was no stopping what came next. I slammed the brakes hard, but the rain-slick pavement turned my tires into skates. My Candy Apple Red 300ZX—Levi's gift, my pride—slid straight under the trailer like it was being swallowed whole. Metal crunched, glass shattered, and all I could do was grip the wheel and brace for impact.

I was furious. Beyond words. Not just at the wreck, but at myself—for letting it happen. For zoning out. For not seeing it coming. And then came the dread. How was I supposed to explain this to Levi? He didn't just buy me that car—he gave it to me as a symbol. A reward for surviving the chaos, for pushing through the fire. And now it was gone. Just like that.

Because of the speed I was going, I had torn the roof of the 300ZX clean off. There was no damage to the trailer at all. Even though I was hurt physically and emotionally, I could not shake the thoughts of my godfather recently dying from AIDS.

I refused to go to the hospital. I'd spent too much of my youth in sterile rooms and under fluorescent lights—no way I was going back unless I had no choice. Levi was heated at first, but once he saw I was walking and talking, relief softened the edge. I told him everything—why my head wasn't in the moment, how Chey had been weighing heavy on me that morning. If he was still upset after that, he didn't let it show. Even with my first car wrecked and the adrenaline still fading, my mind wasn't on the crash. It was on Chey. Still was.

My godfather Chey used to drink all day every day, and it is safe to say that alcohol was his water. He would always say, "Pump....Pump.... Pump It Up," when he flexed his muscles. When I was younger, he used to hold out his arms and let all the kids grab onto his arm and swing. One time, my mother told me that Chey had allowed a car to drive over his chest. After the car had driven over his chest, he got up off the ground mad at the car because it drove over him, although he told them to.

Chey's mother's name was Ms. Joann, and she was not only a mother to him, but also to my father. Growing up in those days, people had their natural parents, but they also had neighborhood parents. Chey's favorite saying was, "I'm Grandmaster Flash and The Furious Five!" And he said that whenever he flexed his muscles, which was often. Chey was my got damn nigga!

Yeah, I always used to sit around and think about my homies and friends, and Chey was one of them that I thought of often. Chey was one of those individuals who stayed drunk from dusk until dawn, but guess what? People still did not play games with him. He was about 6ft and 300 lbs. of solid muscle, and if you came at him the wrong way, he would make you feel all 300 lbs. of it.

My father Levi had a whole crew of friends—some I liked, some I just vibed with. He knew so many people that sometimes I catch myself wondering where they all ended up, what paths they took. One name that always comes to mind is Mr. Prince, the hack-man. I still remember a conversation we had—one of those moments that sticks with you, even years later.

Strangely he said to me "when there is too much of a product in circulation, it causes the price or value of that product to go down." I remember him saying, "Will, take heed to what I am telling you. The more you are seen and heard from, the more common you appear. If you are already established in a group, it would be good for you to temporarily withdrawal from it. If you decide to withdraw temporarily, it will cause you to be talked about or even admired more. You must learn when to leave or fold. Will you need to create value through scarcity?"

After my accident and talking with Levi, I sat and watched my grandmother's health continue to decline. Grandma Inas did her best to help with Grandma Laura by clothing her, feeding her, and simply being a good friend.

One day I caught both of my grandparents sitting in the living room talking and seeing them both engaged in their conversation was like the perfect picture of them together. People say a picture is worth 1000 words. Well, in this case, it would have been worth a ten thousand words if I would have taken a picture. I could not help but think that with every passing day, my grandmother's health was deteriorating. There were times when Grandma Laura would complain about not being able to see. And of course, she continued to talk about the man in the backyard digging a hole for her. I hated her saying that shit with everything I had.

What she said had me so frustrated, I finally stepped out back just to see if I was missing something—maybe some kind of construction going on that I hadn't noticed. I stood there at the door, scanning the yard like it held answers. And then, out of nowhere, I started laughing. Not because anything made sense, but because I remembered all the ridiculous stuff that had gone down out there over the years. That yard had seen some wild moments.

I remembered one time when my cousin Travis asked me for a dog chain. The funny part was I already had a dog chain. I just had to get it for him.

"How long I have to wait before you get it," Travis asked.

"Give me one second," I told him, then headed to my backyard.

Now get this—I had a dog that passed maybe three months before Travis came asking for a damn dog chain. So what do I do? I grab a shovel and head out back, thinking I buried the dog near the fence. I start digging where I was sure the spot was. Nothing. Just dirt. I move over, dig another hole. Still nothing. I keep going—hole after hole—like some lunatic chasing bones. No dog. No chain. Just me, standing in a yard full of craters, wondering if I imagined the whole damn thing.

It was like *Pet Cemetery*. I was thinking, *how in the hell did this dog disappears?* After digging all those holes, a few of my friends were outside with me, watching me as I dug up the entire yard.

If I found the chain, Travis was going to give me $15 for it. As stupid as this may sound, $15 was a lot of money to me back then. By the time I had looked up from all the holes I had dug in my parent's yard, I had forgotten about my parents coming home. All I heard was, "Boy what are you doing?" My father's voice boomed out from behind me. His voice caused me to freeze from fright, with the shovel still in hand. I know my homeboys were thinking, *it's about to go down!*

"What's this stupidity you're doing," Levi continued.

"Travis said he would pay me $15 if I sold him my dog chain." My dumb ass tried to rationalize with him, but there was no rationale behind this. I simply needed to make a few bucks.

"What does a dog have to do with you out here digging up this yard like this?"

"Three months ago, I buried my dog deep in the yard somewhere."

Levi looked at his yard, taking in all the holes and back at me, then back at the yard once again. "Now one more time please, explain again."

This time taking in a few deep breaths, "Three months ago I buried a dog in the back yard. Travis said he needed a job; I mean a dog chain. I told him I had just one chain, but it was in the backyard, and I'd need to dig it up—"

If you had to guess, you'd know I didn't finish—Levi slapped me before I could finish. However, he not only slapped the shit out me, but he slapped the childhood memories out me in front of all my friends and knocked me to the ground.

"Look at my damn yard. Will for you to be the oldest, you truly seem to be the dumbest child I have," he said standing over of me while I lay on the ground. And at this point, I realized my best bet for survival was to stay on the ground. If I stood up, I'd probably just end up back down there again. I learned my lesson from watching Tucker not stay down.

Travis never paid me for my deeds; I thought to myself as I snapped back to reality and realized I was still standing at the back door reminiscing.

"Boy, what are you doing by the back door? You been standing there it seems like for hours," Grandma Inas asked from the living room.

"I was just thinking, but do you need anything?

"Yeah, I need you to go to the store and get me a pack of More Menthol Cigarettes. You know, the green pack."

I never did like buying cigarettes for my grandparents or anybody else for that matter. I said, "Grandma, you don't need any cigarettes. Look at what those things did to Grandma Laura."

"Boy if you don't get up and buy me some cigarettes, I'm going to kill you," she said it with a look capable of killing me if I stayed there any longer.

Of course, walking to the corner store on Riggs and Monroe, I thought to myself, *why can't she see what them cigarettes do to you? Some people don't believe poop stinks until they smell it.* That's when I got a page from Test on my beeper. I knew it was him because I recognized the house number.

After I came out of the store from getting my grandma's cigarettes, I got another page from Test. This time he entered '911,' which of course is the universal number for an emergency. Being I was directly by the pay phones on Monroe and Riggs, I called him back to see what the so-called emergency was.

"Yo man what's up," Test answered on the first ring. "I need you to get me from the Avenue and take me to Mondawmin if you can."

"You geeking boy, what you think I'm a hack or something," I responded back to him. "Another thing you need to stop using 911 for petty shit. And I hope your ass got some gas money?"

"Well, that's why I need you to take me to Mondawmin to rob the store!"

"What?"

"Look at your scared ass," he said jokingly.

But still, I knew I could not put anything pass this nigga again, especially after what he did to shorty over in Cappuccinos.

"I'm on my way, but don't be doing no foolish shit either." Hanging up the phone, I figured my grandmother could wait for her damn cigarettes. Test knew I had a new car because he saw me around the way with my Grey *1993 dark tint windows Lexus*, with the classic rims on it. My father was working with a man who was selling the car for $1,500, but I only paid $1,000 for it. You know I have to put a booming system in it.

Back at my house and in my car, it only took me ten minutes to get to Pennsylvania Avenue. When I pulled up to his location, I hit the horn and Test came out. Meanwhile, as he was getting in the car, I popped in my D.J Boobie Track 8 Club-mix and turned the shit up. I didn't dance or geek in the car because everyone in the hood saw that as a sign of weakness.

"Man change this shit. Pop in some Scarface," said Test, taking no time once in the car.

"Ok! Ok! I got you!" I said popping in the cassette tape. We kept it gangsta the whole way to the mall.

"I need to go to the second-floor entry," he said as we pulled into the mall lot entrance. "Hold up right here," he quickly said as he jumped out and walked into the second floor of the mall.

As I sat in the car, I caught a glimpse of this girl named Trisha from Walbrook.

And man, she still had an ass—nothing seemed different since school let out a few weeks back.

"Trishaaaa!" I yelled, giving her no choice but to hear me. At this point in my life, I had started to perfect my pimping game. And yes, I started to consider myself what you might call a player. And yes, the ladies loved me.

Trisha was dark skinned, had her hair in a wrap, and had ok tits, but her ass was so damn phat. It was phat enough to be in one of those 2 *Live Crew* videos.

Man, when she turned to see who was calling her, her ass continued to turn as it was on the back of a semi-tractor trailer. She should have a sticker which read, *caution: this truck makes wide turns.* To top it off, she had on a cheetah-print mini-skirt. She walked up to the driver side window and leaned in, folding her arms down on the windowsill.

"Will, where you about to go?"

"I'm going to fuck you I hope?"

"Boy you know you cannot handle this!" She said with a laugh, emphasizing 'the cannot.'

I returned the smile, "But for real, though, Wuz-up with you? Where you off to, boo?"

"Well, you know how I get down! It's Friday, so I came up to Mondawmin to get an outfit for The Paradox tonight." 31

"Before you hit up the club, can I come holla at you," I asked as I went to pinch at her legs.

"Boy, don't you talk to my girl Lisa?" She said pushing my hand away.

"Come on now. You know I don't mess with no damn Lisa. I'm trying to catch up with you for real."

"Here boy, take my number. Nobody's at my house," she said as she shifted her weight to one leg to write her number down on a piece of paper. My eyes shifted to her tits which were popping out.

Taking the piece of paper from her, I told her, "I'm waiting on my man. He ran in the mall to grab something. So take my number and maybe I'll let you eat this dick later on."

"You don't know me do you? I don't have to wait till later. I can do it now!"

And of course, my next words were, "You Bluff'n, and if you not, GET ON

IN!"

Trisha said, "Come On, Hurry Up Before We Get Caught!" As she hopped into the car, I unzipped my zipper, and Trisha went to work right on the Mondawmin lot. I pulled out her titties to accompany the blowjob. It was becoming the perfect day for me, as she had on the mini skirt which was like an invitation to finger popping her. While she was sucking me off at the mall's entrance, I wrote down my number for her. No question about it, I wanted to hook up with her. Yet, she knew I was messing around with her best friend, but obviously, she did not care, and neither did I. I slid my number in her back pocket because her hands and mouth were too busy at the moment to take it from me. I took the luxury to lean my seat back and enjoy Trisha's mouth services.

It was not long before Test ran out of the mall, money in one hand and jewelry in the other. He opened the door, grabbed Trisha by her hair and slung her ass out of the car onto the ground.

"GET THE HELL OUT OF HERE!" He yelled. With him snatching a fine ass chick out the car and seeing the money and jewelry in his hands, I did not ask any questions. I put my little man back where he belonged, put the car in drive, and dipped off out of the parking lot doing about 40 mph.

A few minutes out of the mall's parking lot, I finally had the nerve to ask what was going on. That's when he told me he'd robbed someone in the mall's bathroom not long before. My first thoughts were, *WHAT THE HELL! This nigga done messed my good day all the way up. And poor Trisha getting dragged out of the car like a Hebrew slave.*

"Nigga, how you are getting head while I'm inside robbing a mutha fucka," Test said laughing his ass off.

"You done lost your fucking mind! And you done messed up my coochie shot for tonight," I said.

"Man fuck that nasty hoe. I'll get you another one Nigga!"

"Well, there ain't no getting another one of these," I said smiling before putting my fingers I had up in Trisha to Test's nose.

"Man, if you don't get that shit away from me," he said, smacking my hand away. He did not think it was funny, but after ruining my talk with Trisha, I did not care.

After I had dropped Test off, I headed home. Pulling up in front of the house I remembered I still had my grandmother's cigarettes, and I knew she was going to fuss me out once I got in there, asking, *"Where have you been all this time. With all that time I could have walked myself to the store?"* Yeah, Yeah, same ole, same ole.

I dropped Test back off at Pennsylvania Avenue, and ten minutes later I was parking the car back in front of my house. Still in the car, I looked around and noticed **The Hole** was live. People were everywhere outside having fun. Some folks had their grills out on the front doing their grilling thing. Others had card games going. I looked further down the street, and I saw a dice game going on. I thought to myself, *craps for sure.* Them street dudes all about the dollar. Across the street, the little kids were playing jump rope. Finally, in the middle of the street, my cousin Destiny had all her home girls on the block, and they were dancing to music coming from my Aunt B's house.

With the car parked I went into the house and gave my Grandma Inas her cigarettes without any yelling from her, meaning she must have been in a good mood. I went down to the basement and brought out my DJ equipment I'd been experimenting with over the past few months. As I was bringing up my equipment and sitting it out front, my Grandma Inas asked me, "What you about to do a party?"

I paused and thought about it for a moment, as I had yet to throw a party. I nodded my head and said, "Yes ma'am, right here on the front."

It was time for me to do my thing. Once I got everything hooked, up the first thing I put on was Eric B & Rakim's, "Thinking of a Master Plan." Simply thinking about this, I can picture that sunny day and the music playing. *"I'm thinking of a master plan, it ain't nothing but sweat inside my hand."* I knew this would get everybody's attention and would get the girls to all flock around me.

The first question they asked me was, "how much you charge for a party," and "Can you do my party?"

And of course, I always responded with something related to sex, such as, "I will do your party for free if we can have an orgy?" If they never said no about it, I knew they were down for it or at least considered it. After a few more questions I got more serious on the two turntables.

Throwing on hit after hit, more people started to sit around on the nearby steps and listen to me. My brother Nick and his friend Tim came out of the alley and watched me do my thing on the ones and two's. Not long after, everybody came out—Quick, Nate, Tydy, Six, Tucker, Tricks, Cruddy, Obie, Midget, Nelson, Rue, Corey, and K'mar all pulled up with every hood chick we knew for the unofficial outside block party I had kicked off.

The energy was so live, people from other neighborhoods and blocks heard the music and came through to the block party. We partied until Levi came and told me to turn the music off so Grandma Laura could get some rest.

Once I shut off the music, everyone started complaining and yelling the DJ is bullshit. But it was all good; I knew they were joking—they'd been out there for hours just listening to me spin on the turntables. More importantly, they knew I was not willing to go up against Levi. He was known around the neighborhood for being somebody who did not put up with people's shit.

When I stopped the music, other houses turned on their radios, and it kept going. People dispersed, but I wasn't upset—I actually wanted to mingle, especially with all the new girls who had walked into the neighborhood.

After I had brought my equipment back into the house, I gave my grandmother a kiss and told her I was sorry for the noise. Rushing out of the house to meet everyone, I dropped my pager. Picking it up I noticed I had two pages from the same unknown number. So, of course, I went back into the house and called the number back.

"Hello, did anybody page Will?" I asked.

"Is this Will?" the feminine voice answered back.

"Yeah, this Will, who is this? Is this Trisha?"

"That's fucked up how I suck your little dick and your homeboy gonna throw me out the car like it wasn't nothing. And you went along and pulled the fuck off!"

I was thinking, *Damn, I forgot all about that.* "Baby I'm so sorry. I didn't know he was going to do what his crazy ass did!"

"You better tell his ass he doesn't know who he is messing with," she continued as I pictured her rolling her eyes and waving her finger around.

I was thinking, *Damn this bitch crazy.* I didn't think she would call me back after, and I wanted to hang up since I wasn't in the mood to be fussed out. But I felt bad for her being dragged out of the car, and on top of this, the blow job was damn good too. So, I let her vent over the phone. When she finished cussing at me, I said, "girl what time you want me come get you?" Yeah, I was arrogant and sure of myself.

"Who said I wanted you to pick me up?" she said, trying to snap back.

"Girl stop playing games, you know you like the way this dick taste," I said seductively. "Are you still going down to the Dox tonight?"

"Well, if you come get me I won't." She said more calmly. And with that, I knew I was in.

"What time?" I asked.

"Around 10:00 pm."

"Ok, I will call you when I'm on my way."

Right after I hung up the phone with her, my mind jumped straight to one thing—getting some "New New." That was my personal code for hooking up. And in my book, the only thing better than fresh company... is double the trouble.

I went back outside with the others and found the party was still jumping. I looked at my watch, and it read 7:37 pm. I had two hours before I had to get Trisha's phat ass.

Outside, Midget looked at me and said, "Blackbird where you been?" I gave him a look thinking, *who are you calling Blackbird?* He followed by saying, "My fault, it's D.J Blackbird."

I started thinking, *OOH, this man just gave me my D.J name. I like it. D.J Blackbird.* Me and Midget went over with the girls to talk to them. One of the girls by the name of Tiffany asked me, "Will why do you walk like that?"

I responded, "I walk with a limp 'cause my dick is heavy, and I like if from the back so hold your butt steady." Everybody around us started laughing as they loved the answer. Tiffany threw her soda at me in a joking manner. *Oh Yeah*, with a playful toss, she instantly was put on my sex list. I made sure to take a mental note of it.

Soon after, my back started hurting me, so I walked back to the house and took my pain medication, 512mgs of Percocet. While walking back to the house, I started thinking; maybe I should get a hotel and get Trisha to rub my entire body down. I looked at the sky for rain clouds, as my body would always start to ache before it rained. For some reason, my body did it regularly; I considered it my personal forecaster.

The night rolled on with folks hanging out, kicking back in **The Hole** like usual. But where there's good vibes, trouble's never far behind. Somewhere deep into the evening, my cousin Charles and his brother David went from joking to full-on brawling—no holds barred, like they were out for blood. I still don't know what Charles did to set David off, but whatever it was, it lit a fuse. Next thing I know, David's got a shovel in hand, and he's smashing out every window in Charles' car like it owed him money.

Charles was furious—livid that his brother had wrecked his prized all-black Cadillac Deville. Like everything else in the hood, that car wasn't just transportation; it was a statement. Light tint on the windows, chrome glinting off the rims—it was his pride. But by the time David was done swinging that shovel, the Deville looked like it had survived a riot. Headlights shattered, windshield cracked, side mirror dangling, hood and trunk dented, brake lights busted.

It was carnage. Charles didn't hesitate. He snatched a baseball bat and cracked it across David's back with everything he had. Lucky for David he was built like a linebacker—any less muscle and Charles might've snapped bones instead of just making a point.

After about fifteen minutes of straight-up chaos—fists flying, tempers flaring—someone finally had the sense to call the cops. The Western District station was just four blocks east on Riggs, so it didn't take long. Sirens started wailing, and David got amped like it was showtime. Charles, still fired up, stepped into the middle of the street and dared him to settle it like men—bare knuckles, no weapons.

And then it happened. If I didn't know better, I'd swear fifty squad cars came flooding into **The Hole** from every direction—North Riggs, South Riggs, even storming up the 1000 block of Appleton like it was a full-blown raid. The cops didn't waste time. David got cuffed for wrecking Charles' Cadillac, and Charles got hauled off for swinging that bat like he was in the World Series.

The Hole was deep; there were people everywhere. People were looking out their home windows, standing and sitting on their steps, or just standing around. When the police finally left, the crowd started to disperse. I walked off with Tydy because he said the girl named Jasmine on Monroe Street was trying to go around Cappuccinos. With all the sex action I was trying to get, I should have been a porn star.

When we arrived on Monroe Street, Jasmine and her cousin Lorrell were posted on the front steps. Lorrell wasn't exactly a head-turner in the usual sense, but she had a little something going on in the back, and that earned her a few points in my book. I was just looking to kill time until 10:00 p.m., so I kept it moving.

First, I got some head on Mondawmin's parking lot, well let's say by the entrance of the mall. Now I was about to get some action from Lorrell in Cappuccino's; afterward, I was going to go freaking with Trisha. Life was good!

Tydy and I took our time, walking the ladies over to where things were about to go down. Once we got to Cappuccino's, the vibe shifted instantly—no hesitation, just straight into party mode. Tydy handled his business with both Lorrell and Jasmine, and I wasn't far behind. But what really caught me off guard was when the two of them turned their attention to each other. That twist? I didn't see it coming.

"What the Hell!" I asked them, "aren't y'all cousins or some shit? And Y'all doing this to each other?"

They answered, "We're not cousins. We only call each other cousins."

My man Tydy with his funny ass, said, "I don't care what the hell Y'all are, we only want the booty," getting us to laugh.

Man, it had been a minute since I'd stepped foot in Cappuccino's. Back in the early '90s, you couldn't tell me anything—girls in the neighborhood were throwing themselves at us like it was some kind of trend. And truth be told, I wasn't complaining. If I could get mine six hundred times a day, I was good.

I was like Tydy, "I don't give a hell. I simply want the booty!"

«««« ♠♠ »»»»

Later on in the evening night after my little rendezvous with Jasmine and Lorrell, my mother asked me to come up her church and help her with a few things. I did not have much to do until 10 pm, so why not?

Mom told me she wanted me to come to the church to help her pick up some canned goods they were giving away. While helping them load the canned goods into a van, I learned it happened to be rehearsal night for the church choir. After I had stopped in to hear them practice, I met this girl on the choir named Teresa

The first thing which ran through my mind about her was that *I got another victim*. When I saw her walk away by herself it was a go for me, I followed her and said, "Hey Teresa I'm the pimp!"

She turned and looked at me like I had some crawling on my face and said, "WHAT!!!"

I told her to come closer, when she came closer, I repeated myself, "Teresa I am The Pimp."

"You stupid," she said laughing.

Whenever a girl laughs at my jokes, for some reason it means she wants to be mine.

I gathered up all the canned goods, and after a little small talk with Teresa, I told my mother I was about to leave. When Teresa asked, "Why don't you come to church?"

"Why don't you be my baby mother?" I responded, which of course got her to laugh once again.

I thought myself to be a P.I.M.P for sure, and if it meant I had to go to church to get laid by another girl, well *Brother Levi Carter III* will become a Deacon.

Sorry God but you made women. Nobody told you to make women with incredibly sexy features. OOOPS! I meant incredible creatures. God if you had made Will and Jill instead of Adam and Eve, I would have had Jill ass doing everything slutty, and she would not have had time to eat from the damn tree. Not only would I have eaten apple but the grapes, the coochie, the peaches and everything else. Why did you make it so good if you did not want a man to eat it? That's like putting a bone before a dog and command the dog not to eat it. How do you think that's going to work out?

At this point, I loved God with all my heart, but I thought he was trying to set us men up at times. I told my mother if she ever needed any more canned goods picked up, she could call me. She thanked me and said, "You think you some lover."

"Well, God made me," I responded.

I gave Teresa a hug before I did my George Jefferson and stroll out of the church. I went back around my way, and Tucker wanted me to take him down to my cousin Murphy's house on Pulaski Street and Edmondson Avenue. I was not up for it, but it's my brother, and I did not want to make a fuss like I do with my homies, so I drove him. Every time I go down to Murphy's house, all I ever think about is Murphy father, R.I.P Yancy. Even though it was good to see my Aunt Skylar and my cousin's Hailey, Orenda and Murphy. I still missed Yancy!

I'm doing my best to give my son a clear, honest answer to what seemed like a simple question. But the truth is, it's not just about answering—it's about making sure he truly understands. And the only way I knew how to do that was by writing this first book in a series of five.

www.ingramcontent.com/pod-product-compliance
Lightning Source LLC
Chambersburg PA
CBHW051208120626
46547CB00013B/1256